Britain's Glory,
Charlotte:
The People's Princess

By Wayne Goodman

Originally published through Kindle Direct as an electronic book in 2013

First paperback printing, February 2015

Copyright © 2012 by Wayne Goodman

All rights reserved. No part of this book may be reproduced, scanned, or distributed in any printed or electronic form without permission. Please do not participate in or encourage piracy of copyrighted materials in violation of the author's rights. Purchase only authorized editions.

wayne goodman books

waynegoodmanbooks@gmail.com
Twitter: @WGoodmanbooks

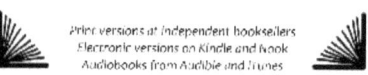

Print versions at independent booksellers
Electronic versions on Kindle and Nook
Audiobooks from Audible and iTunes

Version 1.75
4 May 2015

ISBN: 978-0-9888143-1-8
Library of Congress Control Number: 2013905078

I first learned of The Princess Charlotte Augusta of Wales when reading a book about her cousin, Queen Victoria. The author had wanted the reader to have a fuller understanding of the events leading up to Victoria's coronation in 1837, and no one had a greater impact on Victoria's ascension to the British throne than Princess Charlotte.

This often-overlooked young woman could have been a long-serving monarch under different circumstances. As things worked out, Charlotte never got the chance to fulfill the role for which she was born.

Because of the amazing resources available chronicling the historical period, I have been able to include actual quotations and first-hand observations. A Glossary of unfamiliar names and terms is at the end.

Also, I could not have created this edition without the dedication and perseverance of my friend Jericho Wilson. Thank you does not say enough.

This version is dedicated to Princess Charlotte Elizabeth Diana, born 2 May 2015 to Prince William and Duchess Catherine. May her life be as fulfilling as her namesake but much, much longer.

ARGUMENT

A FEW YEARS before the Rebellion of the American Colonies, King George III of Great Britain worked with Parliament to establish a set of guidelines for Royal Marriages. His brother, Prince Henry, Duke of Cumberland and Strathearn, had married a divorced commoner, Mrs. Anne Horton. This displeased the King greatly because he wanted to maintain a standard of purity in his descendants' bloodline.

According to the Royal Marriages Act of 1772 (12 Geo 3 c. 11), no descendant of George II, male or female, could marry without consent of the reigning monarch. Any marriage contracted without the express consent of the monarch was to be null and void. (This provision remains in effect today, and princes and princesses of this line, no matter in which country they may reside, still seek the approval of the British monarch before marriage.)

During the Autumn of 1788, King George III suffered a bout of porphyria, a hereditary kidney malfunction that causes porphyrins to accumulate in the bloodstream rather than be excreted. This can lead to nervous system dysfunction, and the King appeared mentally ill during the course of the disease. Parliament argued over whether Prince George of Wales should become Regent during the King's inability to rule. The Whig Party, behind Charles James Fox, supported the regency. Prime Minister William Pitt (the Younger), leader of the Tories, opposed the regency. Before Parliament could reach a decision, King George recovered and resumed his regular duties.

3 November 1817, Claremont House, Surrey
Evening

On a clear day it was possible to see Windsor Castle to the northwest and the great dome of St. Paul's Cathedral to the northeast from the high knoll in the garden. This, however, was an overcast autumn evening, and very little could be seen in the dim light of rural Esher.

Claremont House, the royal home of Princess Charlotte and Prince Leopold, anticipated a blessed event set into motion 20 years prior. Lights burned at some windows, and others remained dark with drawn drapes. Very few people had seen the Princess during the later stages of her pregnancy. Charlotte had already endured two known miscarriages in attempting to produce a royal heir. This was the first time she had been able to carry to term.

"Stocky! Stocky!" swarthily handsome, 27-year-old Leopold screamed as he ran through the halls, searching for his physician, friend and confidante, Baron Christian Stockmar. "The baby! It's finally arriving!"

1795, office of Prime Minister William Pitt (the younger), Westminster, London
Afternoon

Prince George strode back and forth in front of the desk as the seated Prime Minister's eyes followed each pace.

"Damme, Pitt! You have opposed me at every turn."

"Your Highness, I have only been performing the job to which I have been elected." Pitt's coolness had no effect on the Prince's hot temper.

"I need more funds!"

"To purchase more of Beau Brummel's extravagant wardrobe or to pay down your ever-mounting debts?" The Prime Minister began reviewing his evening plans in his mind. *Boodle's or White's?* "I have heard things have gotten to such a sorry state that your exorbitant allowance no longer covers even the interest on your borrowings."

George stopped and pointed a pudgy finger at Pitt. "That is none of your business, sir."

Pitt glanced down at his own fingers, "That is all of my business, Your Highness." He looked up and directly into the Prince's squinting eyes. "Your family is not exactly popular with the populace at this time. Among all of your multitude of brothers and sisters there is not one legitimate heir for the next generation."

"I don't know what you mean. Most of us have borne children." He began to pace again.

"None of which are legal heirs according to your father the King. Must I recite the Royal Marriages Act for you?"

"The old fool doesn't even know which of his own children are his."

Pitt spooned sugar into the teacup in front of him. "Your mother the Queen still has her faculties, and, despite public opinion, I do believe I still possess mine." He reached for the teapot and filled his cup. "Without His Majesty's approval, none of your lot's spouses, or their issue, are legitimate." A surreptitious motion added a splash of his favourite gin to the tea from a small phial hidden in his sleeve.

"Where am I going to find the money to cover my next payment? My creditors are hounding me." He drew a lace-edged silk cloth from his sleeve and dabbed at his sweaty face.

"Your Highness," he paused to take a sip of tea "we have already granted you over £200,000 to cover your debts and repair your residence." Another sip. "There is nothing more Parliament can do given the current situation."

George tamped the silk cloth back into his sleeve. "Situations change."

"Indeed they do, Your Highness, indeed they do." A bit more tea.

"Do you mock me, sir?" the Prince glared.

Pitt stared back, "It is not my place to mock Your Highness. It is my place only to advise Your Highness of available options. If you wish the government to allot you even more money," he looked away to find the teacup and take another sip, "marry proper and produce a legitimate heir." He then swallowed the rest of the tea. "Now, if you'll excuse me, I must return to my official duty of running this country for your rather overindulgent family."

"Damme, Pitt!" the Prince pounded his fist on the Prime Minister's desk, rattling the teacup. "What must I do to gain your Tory approval? Shall I bring on a Whig uprising?"

Pitt glanced down at the disturbed teacup, "You and your brood of siblings have suckled at Britannia's teat for so long and so hard that she is just about dry, Your Highness." He looked up to meet the Prince's stern face. "I fear that if this abuse of the Royal Treasury continues, there will be nothing left to raise future generations. Observe the French manner of dealing with unpopular royalty."

George turned to leave, "To hell with you, Pitt!"

As the Prince reached for the doorknob, the Prime Minister stated, "As I have already indicated, Your Highness, there might be a way for Parliament to see a rise in your allowance should you marry proper and produce a legal heir."

The Prince turned, "I am married, man! I have children galore."

"None of which are acceptable to your father the King. That includes your whorewife."

George raised his fist menacingly, "How dare you address me in such a common manner, sir!"

"The truth is what it is, Your Highness," Pitt murmured. "Your somewhat clandestine marriage is not recognised by the Monarch. You must follow the dictates of your father's wishes and marry someone more... suitable. That divorced Catholic widow courtesan does not qualify as such, Your Highness."

"There is no one adequately suitable in His Majesty my father's eyes."

"The names of two of your cousins have come to my attention as acceptable spouses," Pitt delivered the information as if casually rolling dice.

"One damned German *frau* is as bad as another," George spat.

The Prime Minister inhaled and exhaled to regain some composure. "One damned *frau* is your mother's niece, Princess Louise of Mecklenburg."

"One of that line is more than enough," he snorted. "Who else?"

"On your father's side, Princess Caroline of Brunswick is available and, bless her, willing."

"I will not marry that fat sow!" The Prince grabbed the knob again and pulled the door.

Pitt muttered, "As you wish, Your Highness. The door is open and now you must choose whether or not to pass over the threshold."

The Prince indicated the door frame with a finger, "That woman could not fit through the opening, Sir."

"If you will excuse me, I must return to more pressing matters." He turned to open a desk drawer.

"I shall see you in Hell, Pitt!" George spat as he stomped out.

"My expectation as well, Your Highness." Pitt took a snort of gin from the hidden phial.

Charlotte: The People's Princess

3 November 1817, Claremont House, Surrey
Evening

"Calm down, Leo," Stockmar purred, "You shall give yourself an apoplectic fit." The Baron, while not as handsome as his companion, stood a bit taller and radiated calmness, even during this stressful time.

Leo paced short distances zigzagging, "Nothing must go wrong, Stocky!"

"Nothing will go wrong," Stockmar followed his friend.

"This is the first time Charlotte has made it this far along. Our baby is the hope of the nation. Stock markets and betting parlours await the outcome all too eagerly. I hear the current book is 2½% rise if it's a Princess, 6% for a Prince."

Stockmar unsuccessfully attempted to put his hand on the kinetic Leopold's shoulder. "The best physicians in England are looking after her. She's in good hands."

Prince Leopold stopped and turned to face Stockmar, "Those fakirs have no idea what they are doing to my wife! You are the only one who should be tending to her, not that assemblage of boobs her father has chosen."

"I shall call for Sir Richard. He will handle things from here."

Leopold began pacing anew, "Croft better know what he's doing. My future is in his hands!"

Carlton House

7 January 1796, Carlton House, London
Late morning

Expectant father Prince George stood surrounded by his entourage in the drawing room of the palatial home he designed for himself. An elegant and splendid residence, decorations of china and bronze ornaments hung from the richly-paneled walls.

He held his hands tucked into the small of his back, pushing forward his emerging gut. George believed he was as debonair as the flattering portraits which hung on the walls. To others, he was fatter and more plain. Those who wished to remain in his circle of friends supported his self-impressed beliefs.

"Yes, George would be the obvious choice, but we have so many Georges already." He laughed out loud and his followers joined in. "Perhaps we should go with Charles, after my mother, or–dare I say it–Arthur, for that truly dignified approach." The Prince tugged at his lapel and burst forth, "Perhaps I should just say Beau Brummel and hope for future discounts!"

Charlotte: The People's Princess

The crowd erupted in laughter as a nurse approached and whispered into the Prince's ear.

"Daughter?" he looked about with a grimace. "A daughter?!?" Prince George bellowed as the nurse shied away, "I had to get royally pissed to impregnate that foul-smelling cow, and this is how she repays me? A fucking daughter?"

People in the room turned to stare at the distraught new father.

"And Princess Caroline of Brunswick was no virgin, I tell you verily," he paused to survey the crowd. "I am not aware of how many other 'gentlemen' the Princess had the opportunity to pleasure before we wed, but she did confide that my royal member was quite substantial." He strode to the liquor table and poured another whiskey.

The onlookers turned their faces away as George began to laugh at his own joke.

"Only the King, Himself, will be pleased with this unwelcome turn of events!" He spat on the floor. "A girl child means *nothing* for me, nothing *more* for me." George began to down the liquor.

"Congratulations, Your Highness," the Archbishop of Canterbury entered from the accouchement room and approached George. John Moore had an egg-shaped body with a friendly round face set on top. "As you indicated, she is a rather fine child! Do you wish to know the condition of the Princess?"

The Prince turned to the Archbishop, prepared to use unfit language to express his distaste, disinterest and disgust for his wife Caroline, then chose merely to reply, "No, thank you, Your Eminence, that will not be necessary."

Britain's Glory

3 November 1817, Claremont House, Surrey
Evening

Stockmar opened the dark-paneled door of Charlotte's drawing room that had been converted into the accouchement chamber. "Leo!" he yelled out. "Sir Richard suggests we call for the official observers. The time draws nigh! Send a messenger to Windsor immediately! Summon the Privy Councillors!"

The Prince scrambled to the writing desk in his own drawing room and hastily grabbed paper, quill and ink. He scribbled as best he could under the circumstances, blotted the paper, folded it as neatly as he could and handed it to his gentleman. "*Bitte, nehm du diesen Brief an der Königen im Schloss Windsor schell. Danke.*"

As the attendant ran out, Baron Stockmar walked in and grabbed the arm of his friend, feeling the sweat-sopped sleeve. "Leo, it won't be long now."

Leopold half smiled and turned to face his friend, "*Danke, mein freund, vielen Dank.*"

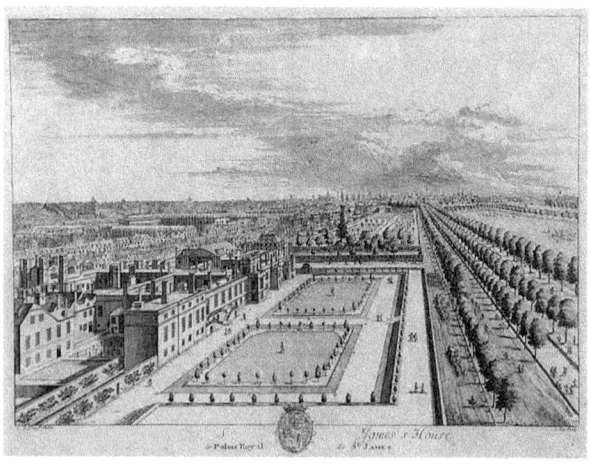

St. James Palace

Charlotte: The People's Princess

11 February 1796, St. James Palace, London
Late morning

King George III, now almost 60 years old and somewhat senile, held his granddaughter over the baptismal font in the Great Drawing Room. Light through the wide windows glowed on the cerulean blue carpet. Even with a head of grey hair, the King retained his handsome, striking Germanic features, his intense blue eyes focused on the infant.

"I christen thee, Charlotte Augusta" the clergyman intoned, "daughter of George Augustus Frederick and Caroline Amelia Elizabeth."

Pudgy and pungent Princess Caroline, the infant's mother, leaned toward Queen Charlotte, for whom the baby was named. "Lady Townshend looks like she is about to topple over. Isn't she with child herself? Perhaps she should sit," she whispered.

"She may stand," the Queen croaked as she dusted the snuff off her fingers, "she may stand." This woman had borne 15 children to King George, of which only 13 survived to adulthood. Her permanent scowl set the lines on her once-smooth face.

The King giggled childishly and grabbed the baby. "My very first grandchild!" he roared, holding up the infant Princess. His sons and daughters in attendance, many of whom had children, but none that their father The King recognised as legitimate heirs, scowled in unison. "Charlotte, my little love!" he proclaimed as he kissed her forehead and dashed out of the hall, toward the balcony overlooking Pall Mall.

"Follow him," screamed Princess Caroline. "Follow him! Get my baby back!"

The King looked over his shoulder at the royal procession in pursuit. "Forget it, Caroline! She is no longer your child. She belongs to Britain now. You shall not see her again!" He rounded the corner and opened the great windows with one hand, the infant Princess tucked in the crook of the other arm.

"Damme, father," Prince George swore to himself, "it's not your child."

"People of Britain," the King announced, "behold your future queen, Charlotte, Princess of Wales."

Londoners who happened to be passing by the Mall stopped to look up at the doddering old man in the window. He was dangling an infant over the railing and screaming nonsense. "Crazy old George," they muttered.

4 November 1817, Claremont House, Surrey
Morning

"His Eminence, the Archbishop of Canterbury, and the Viscount Sidmouth, the Home Secretary, have arrived," Baron Stockmar announced to the frowning Prince Leopold. His wife, Princess Charlotte, had been in labour since the previous evening.

The Prince continued to focus on Charlotte in her chamber, oblivious to his friend's presence. Stockmar tapped Leopold on the shoulder and repeated, "The Privy Council has arrived."

After about a second, Leopold inhaled slowly and responded, "Show them in, show them in, please."

Henry Addington, currently the Home Secretary who once served as Prime Minister, appeared gaunt and bony, a shadow of his former robust profile. Archbishop Charles Manners-Sutton, now toothless and bald, stood hunched and bent. Fortunately for these two senior statesmen, all they were required to do was witness the impending birth and affirm the infant as the true issue of Princess Charlotte.

Leopold returned to the main room and greeted the two official observers, ushering them into the accouchement room, where the

Princess was surrounded by the royal physicians and the accoucheur, Sir Richard Croft.

May 1797, Carlton House, London
Early afternoon

"Princess Caroline, the baby has arrived!" Caroline's lady-in-waiting announced.

The Princess dismissed her personal physician and shuffled toward the apartment's entrance to receive her daughter. She had retained all the weight she gained while pregnant and added a few pounds more. Her German heritage dictated her body shape.

A royal nurse carrying the infant Princess from the Prince's upstairs portion of the palace entered and approached Caroline. She wrinkled her nose as soon as she could smell the mother's unbathed body. German heritage also dictated a style of hygiene which most members of the British Royal Family found intolerable, especially her estranged husband, Prince George. The Prince had changed his will denying Caroline any say over the rearing of their child. However, the mother was afforded the occasional visit because the staff felt it best that the new Princess spend some time with her birth mother. Despite orders to the contrary, they even left little Charlotte alone with Caroline from time to time.

Once the baby's royal attendants had left, Caroline instructed the mews handler to prepare her carriage. "I wish to go shopping at Mayfair, and I want to show off the Princess as well. I believe the weather is fair enough for the top to be lowered. The people should want to see us."

Britain's Glory

As she stood waiting for the carriage, Caroline looked down at the infant in her arms and cooed, "Charlotte, *du bist so ein schönes Mädchen, und eines Tages wirst du sein Königin!*" Then she kissed her daughter on the forehead.

She could barely step up into the passenger compartment. It took two of her ladies to assist her. Even without the added burden of the baby she would have had difficulty.

Caroline ordered the driver to take them through Hyde Park along the way. She wanted to have as many commoners as possible see her with her daughter, now second in line to the throne of Britain. Prince George may have removed Caroline from his life, but she wasn't going to let London forget who brought the royal heir to their life.

As the carriage proceeded on its way to Mayfair, Caroline waved to people on the street, and they waved back. She held the Princess of Wales up for her subjects to see, and people cheered.

"Ha, George!" Caroline said to herself, "people still love me despite your being ever so unpopular." She grinned and continued to wave.

The driver turned back to determine whether the Princess was addressing him. When he realised she was only talking to herself, he rolled his eyes and turned back to his duties.

Princess Caroline glanced down and lectured the baby, "Your father is a pompous, arrogant, ill-mannered boy, and I will make him regret what he gave up and threw away."

The cheering continued all along the way to the shops. People came from blocks around to get a glimpse of the future queen, Princess Charlotte of Wales.

Caroline, was only too happy to oblige them. She enjoyed being fawned over and attended to. While it was not a substitute for her husband's affection, it did feel good. She had other plans for dealing with George's bad behavior.

Charlotte: The People's Princess

4 November 1817, Claremont House, Surrey
Afternoon

Prince Leopold sat alone in the hallway outside Charlotte's drawing room. The drapes were drawn and only a few rays of sunlight passed around the edges.

The connecting door opened and Baron Stockmar approached the Prince, every squeak of the floorboards reverberating off the dark paneling.

Stockmar whispered, "Leo," and he touched the Prince's moist wrist, "things are not going well. I believe the baby is ill-positioned for delivery, and Charlotte's musculature is not developed sufficiently to give birth without assistance."

Sweat beaded on Prince Leopold's forehead. "Stocky, *Ich bin wie die Teufel schwitzen*. I have never been so scared and nervous. Will they make it?"

Stockmar paused to reflect before responding, "I believe the Princess will be fine. I am uncertain, however, as to the fate of the child. Sir

Britain's Glory

Richard will not let her eat anything. I fear that without proper nutrition Charlotte will have difficulties."

Sir Richard Croft had studied with Dr. Thomas Denman, the preeminent physician of his time. According to Dr. Denman, excessive pressure from the expanding uterus endangered the health of the mother. To counteract this perceived deadly threat, Sir Richard enforced a policy of restricting food intake from the beginning of the labour process, and he was not about to alter the plan. Contemporary medical protocol demanded this course of action and he was not going to stray from it.

The Prince paced the darkening hallway next to the drawing room. "Stocky, why are you not taking charge?" Leopold halted and turned to his friend, "It seems you and I are the only two who care for the well-being of the Princess." By this time, his clothing dripped with his nervous sweat.

Stockmar placed his hand on the Prince's wrist, "Croft is a good man, but I am beginning to question his methods."

Buckingham House

4 June 1797, The Queen's House (Buckingham), London
Late afternoon

The Yellow Drawing Room, with its spectacular cylindrical crystal chandelier, hosted members of the Royal Family and their attendants for the King's birthday. The warm day might have encouraged perspiration, and people had dressed more informally. The setting sun cast a few beams through the heavily-curtained window, catching some of the large framed mirrors, creating a golden haze within the obnoxiously yellow brocade-covered walls.

"Miss Hayman," commanded the King, sitting on a red velvet chair next to the white marble fireplace, "bring us our little grandchild. If this is to be a birthday celebration, let the tiny Princess be my present." As requested, the youthful nanny brought Princess Charlotte to her grandfather. "And how are you finding my little treasure, the Princess, madam?"

Not in the custom of having Royalty address her directly or even having to respond, Ann Hayman swallowed, touched her smooth throat and gasped, "She is quite... merry, Your Majesty."

"Merry?" roared the King. "My royal granddaughter is officially rated 'merry' by the nursemaid! Do you hear that everyone?" The assembled crowd turned their heads and nodded their ascent. The King addressed to Miss Hayman once again, "And is that all? Merely merry?"

Embarrassed at the unaccustomed attention, she began to blush. "She is magnanimous as well. At bedtimes she prays, 'Bless Papa, Mama, Charlotte and fleas.'"

"Fleas?" the King questioned.

"Yes, Your Majesty. We have instructed the Princess to pray for her enemies as well, and she believes fleas are the only enemies she has."

George laughed heartily. "Well met. What, what?"

"At times she is also hot-pepper hot, if I may say so, Your Majesty."

King George erupted into a reverberating laugh. "Pepper hot you say? You're looking a bit peppery yourself, madam." He pointed at her blushing. "Please enlighten us of our child's antics."

"Well, Your Majesty, Princess Charlotte is quite headstrong, and when she does not get her way, she kicks. Hard, Your Majesty."

"By Jove, she is a Hanover!" As the crowd chuckled along with the King's jest, he tickled under the baby's chin, and she promptly began weeping loudly.

"There, there, my little one," murmured George, "Let us play on the carpet together." The baby quieted when set on the floor, the King of England beside her, touching her petite hands, kissing her golden locks.

"George, you have done well," the King proclaimed loudly to the Prince standing on the other side of the room amidst his entourage.

"Thank you, Your Majesty," the Prince shouted. "After all, dear father, you chose the poor thing's mother," he confided in those standing around him. "That was the simple part. My contribution to the whole affair was quite distasteful and patently necessary. And thank goodness that it is over!" To which he laughed at his own humour, and then those around him laughed politely.

"I do hope you grow up to be as good natured as your father and as wise as your grandpapa," the King told little Charlotte as he continued to dote on her every motion. "You are a well-loved little princess!"

After a while, Queen Charlotte approached the pair, "Dearest George, I do hate to interrupt your playtime, but the procession of mail coaches has commenced." She took a pinch of snuff and sneezed daintily.

The King looked up, "Well then, Charlotte," then at his granddaughter, "And Charlotte, let us proceed to the balcony

Charlotte: The People's Princess

to review the troops." As he stood he mumbled, "Two Charlottes, how shall I ever manage to keep them proper inside my addled head?"

Queen Charlotte led the troops through the halls and into the Centre Room. When they all entered, she waved her gloved hand at the usher, who then opened the doors to the balcony, but only the King, Queen and Princess Charlotte went outside.

The three Royals stood on the balcony overlooking a parade of mail coaches and a crowd of citizens. As the grown-ups waved at the throng, blew kisses and shouted huzzah, little Charlotte imitated them, much to everyone's delight.

Queen Charlotte leaned into her husband's ear, "Observe how easily our Charlotte takes to the crowd. They just adore her! I do believe, George, she truly will be the people's princess."

Britain's Glory

4 November 1817, Claremont House, Surrey
Early evening

"Is Charlotte going good?" Leopold looked into Stockmar's eyes for a glimpse of hope. "Well?"

"She seems very tired. The labour process is dragging on way too long. Croft says she has not yet dilated sufficiently for birthing the baby."

Leopold sighed. "How much longer, Stocky? *Mir Reißt die Geduld.* How much longer?"

"Patience, my friend, patience." The Baron patted the Prince's hand. "*Die Geduld ist eine bittere Pflanze, die eine süße Frucht hat.*" He struck a finger in the air, "That reminds me, I had a chance to examine the listing of pieces Thomas Bruce brought back with him from Athens."

The Prince looked at his friend without understanding, "What are you talking about, Stocky?"

"The Greek ruins, Leo. The British Museum will have them on display quite soon. Do you wish to go with me to see them?"

Leopold nodded his acknowledgment. "But not until Charlotte and the baby are on firm ground." He wiped some perspiration from his face. "I really do not want to talk about cold Greek stones right now."

"I understand." He touched his friend's shoulder. "But if we do not accomplish this in a timely fashion, the Turks may come and take their treasures back," and he smiled with a hint of mischief. "Perhaps you can write the Earl Elgin and request a private showing."

"Perhaps," Leopold whispered, "perhaps... perhaps..."

June 1805, Warwick House, London
Afternoon

"Lady Elgin," Prince George stated with his usual haughty tone reserved for those times when he had to speak to those he felt beneath him, "I should like to receive your report on my daughter's deportment at this time, before I depart for my Summer travels up country." He gazed around the tattered drawing room of the small house he had assigned to the Princess, mustering up as much patience as he could afford.

"First off, Your Highness, I am Lady de Clifford," the harsh Irish brogue syncopated the air. A rather plain but elegant woman, she had married Edward Southwell, Baron de Clifford, who had died in 1777. "Lady Elgin was removed from service when you relocated the Princess Charlotte to this establishment from your other palace next door." She adjusted her turban slightly. "Miss Hayman neither also."

"How silly of me, madam. I should have recognised the difference at once. Please refresh my memory as to why Lady Elgin is no longer in our employ."

Lady de Clifford put her gloved hand to her mouth, "It's not for me to say, Your Highness, but I do seem to remember you dismissed her because she took your daughter, the Princess, to visit your father, the King, without your express prior permission," and she curtsied to demonstrate respect.

Prince George poked a finger in the air, "Ah, yes, insubordination. Something we need not worry about with you. Are we correct, Lady de Clifford?"

"Yes, Your Highness, we are," and she curtsied again.

"How are you finding Warwick House, my Lady?"

"Well," she coughed with her first covering her mouth, "may I speak frankly with Your Highness?"

"Of course. Prithee be frank always, madam."

"Begging Your Highness's pardon, Warwick is a bit shabby compared to Carlton House. It is wanting in repairs, just about falling to ruin it is, and in particular, the roof leaks in my bed chamber."

"We shall set things a-right when the Royal Purse allows," the Prince promised absent-mindedly.

"Thank you, Your Highness. I should think that your daughter's well-being is paramount."

"Of course, of course," he brushed off, "I have found her of late to be a bit sulky. Now please describe her to me, fully, and without edit."

Lady de Clifford paused thoughtfully then began, "Her Highness, the Princess, is a strong-willed child, a handful, you might say." Prince George nodded. The Lady waited to see if he would respond. He merely stared off, perhaps in thought. She continued, "Her attitude is superior to those around her, but she can be unassuming as well. One day she threw open the door of the room where I was sitting writing, and she danced across the way without so much as a care to close the door behind her. I attempted to explain to the Princess that one should shut the door behind; that it is only proper and civil. She told me if I wanted the door closed, I should ring for the house staff."

After a moment the Prince posed, "Does she interact well with other children, my Lady?"

"She has few friends her own age, most of them the children of the other staff members. Her favourite playmate is your father, His Majesty. And, pardon my saying so, Your Highness, but I observe the Princess acting in a very boyish manner: playing soldier and running with the male children." Lady de Clifford adjusted the fingers of her gloves. "And one time when we was visiting my family in Earl's Court, the news got out that herself was there and a crowd started gathering at the front. The young Princess snuck out the side gate with my grandson George, her habitual partner in crimes, and they went around. They asked what everybody was looking at, and she was surprised to hear that they were after getting a look-see at Princess Charlotte her very self!"

"Has she had much contact with her mother?"

"Not so much since the Princess Caroline has removed to Blackheath, Your Highness."

George cleared his throat loudly, "Thank goodness she has finally shoved off. I would prefer toads and vipers crawling all over my victuals than have to sit at the same table with her ever again."

Lady wrinkled her nose, "I expect the little Princess to have no further unattended interactions with her mother."

"Good. Good. My dear father, the King wishes his little granddaughter to be–how does he put it?–an honour and comfort to her relations, and a blessing to the dominions over which she may hereafter preside. Ugh. So pompous. He never had those kinds of expectations for me," he sighed.

Lady de Clifford raised a finger, "I believe I have a few examples of her character for you." The Prince raised an eyebrow ever so slightly. "When we walk about together," she continued, "Charlotte carries what she calls her 'Beggars' Purse' so that she can give charity to those less fortunate."

"Exemplary, Lady de Clifford, exemplary."

"Also, Your Highness, one evening two of the boys was playing a game of chess, and one yelled 'Checkmate!' and the little Princess turned to me, 'Checkmate? What is that?' I explained the King was in peril and no move would save it from capture by the enemy. Bless her heart, she said back to me, 'That is a bad situation, indeed, for a king. Thank goodness Grandpapa would never be in such a position. As long as he conforms to the laws, the citizens will protect him!'"

George giggled briefly. "Ah, the innocence of youth. And how are her studies proceeding?"

"Very well, Your Highness. Dr. Nott reports she is quite bright and learns quickly. The Princess seems fond of him and eager to please. She is also quite good on the pianoforte. I believe she is rather fond of Mozart."

"That Austrian chappie? Do we not have superlative composers in Britain?"

Lady de Clifford clapped her hands, "She enjoys Haydn and Handel very much as well."

"And thank goodness for that!"

"However, at times I believe she is somewhat bored with her studies."

"What brings you to that conclusion, madam?"

She houghed before responding, "She is frequently after making up names for those what works with her, Your Highness. For your example, she refers to the Reverend Dr. Fisher as 'The Great UP.'"

"The Great UP, you say?" questioned the Prince.

"Yes, Your Highness."

"And why do you believe that is, madam?"

"I believe it is the way he pronounces his station as Bishop, Your Highness."

"And how does His Excellency pronounce his title exactly?"

"Bish-UP. He refers to himself as the Bish-UP of Exeter."

The Prince chuckled. "I see. As I seem to recall, His Majesty appointed that pompous twit to oversee Charlotte's education. I fear the man is a spy rather in my father's employ."

"I cannot dispute that, Your Highness. I have taken notice of him writing in a little black book at times when he is not in the presence of the Princess."

"Well, let him do his worst, I say. I cannot remember a time when I was not under some sort of surveillance."

"Also, she frequently mocks him from behind, making her lower lip protrude, gesticulating in a rather presumptuous manner, imitating his exaggerated style. All rather disrespectful, if you ask me. And, although I did not see it directly, I have heard that once she even grabbed his wig and threw it in the fire."

The Prince laughed to himself. "Who else does dear little Charlotte mock behind their back?"

Lady de Clifford exhaled then continued, "One of the governesses, a Mrs. Udney, gives us all reasons to mock."

"Do tell."

"Perhaps it's not for me to say, Your Highness, but Mrs. Udney is always after a bit of gossip and gin." The Prince snickered. "But it's her little intrigues that are beginning to unnerve me."

"How so, madam?"

"Well, Your Highness," and she drew herself up, "The other day I was about to open a door when the Princess herself ran up and grabbed my hand before I could turn the knob. When I asked what the matter was, she warned me that Mrs. Udney had locked herself in the salon with the art master."

"How utterly inappropriate around young children," the Prince recited, thinking of his own clandestine dalliances. "I am almost hesitant to ask what my dear daughter has dubbed this one."

"Mrs. Nibs, Your Highness."

He giggled boyishly. "How appropriate. My little girl is quite astute for her years."

"Aye, Your Highness. I am loathe to discover what she calls me behind me own back."

"Oh, I shouldn't worry, madam. She is quite fond of you."

"Thank you, Your Highness. I endeavor to do me best."

"I am most assured of that, madam." he turned to leave but then turned back. "Oh, I nearly forgot. While I am away, I do not wish little Charlotte left alone with Caroline or the Queen, and most especially the King. And do try to minimise the amount of time she spends with her aunts and uncles. But the main thing I need from you and the rest of the Princess's attendants is any observation of misconduct by my dear wife, the Princess Caroline. I require adequate grounds for divorce so that I can divest myself of that deadweight and get along with my life."

"Yes, Your Highness. I shall be vigilant." As Prince George started off, she asked, "Did Your Highness wish to see the Princess Charlotte before he departs?"

George turned back to face Lady de Clifford directly, "No, thank you, that will not be necessary," and he turned to leave.

4 November 1817, Claremont House, Surrey
Late evening

> "The labour of her Royal Highness the Princess Charlotte is going on very slowly, but we trust favourably." — Progress report from Sir Richard Croft to the Prince Regent

Leopold paced the hallway. The door of the drawing room opened and Baron Stockmar approached. The Prince stopped long enough to inquire of his friend, "What news, Stocky?"

"Our distinguished visitors grow weary," Baron Stockmar whispered for fear of being overheard.

"News of our Charlotte, I mean," Prince Leopold retorted, "I wish to hear of my wife's condition."

Stockmar hesitated before speaking, "The tidings are not good, Leo."

The Prince turned to face Stockmar directly, "What is happening? What is going on?"

"There is meconium in the water, a sure sign of the baby's distress." Leopold gazed at the floor. "I would have Charlotte take some broth or spirits, but Sir Richard refuses to nourish the Princess until the baby arrives."

"Can you not take over, Stocky?" the Prince implored. "You know what's best."

"I wish that I could, but Sir Richard has command at this time. Besides, he is the expert in this field, not I."

Leopold glanced up at his friend, "I hope you are correct, Stocky, I hope you are correct."

10 Downing Street

1 June 1806, 10 Downing Street, London
Midday

The Pillared Room had to be rearranged to accommodate the anticipated crowd of people. An old dining table sufficed for the officials. Various chairs from throughout the building provided seating, and dappled light through the gauze-covered windows highlighted golden threads in the antique Persian carpet.

On one side of the table sat the noble-faced George Spencer, the Home Secretary; Thomas Erskine, the Lord Chancellor, with his dark, wind-whipped hair; Edward Law, appearing more 17th Century with an elbow-length powdered wig and whitened face, the Lord Chief Justice; and William Grenville, the Prime Minister, still dashing even though almost 50 years old, in the centre. Facing the table sat people from the Court, potential witnesses and servants of Princess Caroline.

"I thank you all for attending this rather delicate investigation into the possible misconduct of Princess Caroline," Thomas Erskine began, "As you can see, neither the Prince nor Princess of Wales is in attendance. Due to the nature of our study, it was felt best that the parties to the complaint should not be present. We hope that their absence allows the various witnesses to speak their truth freely and without reservation." He glanced about the room. "Our first deponent is

Charlotte: The People's Princess

Lady Charlotte Douglas, accompanied by her husband, Sir John. Please approach, madam. I see you have prepared a statement, but in the interest of time, could you please merely state the most important facts. Thank you."

As Lady Charlotte approached, the Lord Chief Justice extended his hand to take the papers from her. The sepia silk gown she had chosen for the day added to her air of muted authority. She turned and sat in the chair to address them all.

"Gentlemen, I did not have the acquaintance of Her Highness until November of 1801, when one day she began parading back and forth in front of our Blackheath residence elegantly dressed in a lilac satin pelisse, primrose-coloured half boots, and a small satin lilac traveling cap faced with sable, accompanied by her lady." She fiddled with her sleeves. "We thought it most peculiar to have the Princess of Wales walking past over and again, and at first we figured she was looking for someone else's home. So we went outside and asked if we could be of assistance to Her Highness. She said she believed I was Lady Douglas and she wanted to see my daughter, whom she had heard–by way of Sir Sidney Smith–was exceedingly beautiful." The Lady surveyed the faces of the assembled magistrates but did not receive any indication, some stared back and others looked away. She decided to continue, "My daughter was not with me at that time; however, I did invite the Princess and her lady inside. We chatted for a while and then Her Highness began making such embarrassing remarks to me such as: Oh! believe me you are quite beautiful; different from almost any English woman. Your arms are fine beyond imagination, your bust is very good, and your eyes, Oh! I have never seen such eyes!"

Some snickers could be heard.

"May I remind you, gentlemen, of the delicate nature of this inquiry. Please attempt to hold your remarks, I beg of thee," Erskine admonished. "Madam, please continue."

"Well, we subsequently received an invite to her Montague House, and we were frequent guests of Her Highness. The following Summer, the Princess paid a call to our home and begged of us to guess her news. After a few minutes of us attempting to tell Her Highness that we would not guess, she blurted out that she was with child—"

"Do you mean to say she was pregnant?" interrupted the Lord Chief Justice in his high-pitched nasal tones.

"It's not for me to determine the Princess's state, Your Honour. All I can tell you is what she told us."

"Pray proceed, Lady Douglas."

"She did not mention directly whom she thought the father was, but she kept hinting that the Prince had paid her a nightly visit a while back and that she would declare him as the father of her child. She also bragged that the milk came up into her breasts so quickly it stained her gowns." Lady Douglas turned her head away and glanced briefly at her husband. She once again faced the dignitaries, "The Princess frequently spoke in a common and familiar manner, but it was her custom and I had become acquainted with it. She often made jests at my expense in front of others, which was quite amusing to Her Highness but painful to me after her constant compliments in private. Her manner was not suited to that of a Lady nor a Princess, in my humble opinion."

"We appreciate your candour, madam. Please continue."

"Soon after, I became with child as well. One day I called upon the Princess unannounced and witnessed her being bled with leeches by her attending physician. It is common knowledge that a woman should not be bled with leeches while pregnant. She told me she had a violent heat in her blood and did not wish to harm the baby. When the time came for me to deliver, Princess Caroline had yet to produce, and she insisted upon being present at my child's birth." At this point, Lady Douglas adjusted the skirt in her lap and then looked up again. "Her manner of loose and flowing dress at that time was not unlike women who are late in pregnancy and wish to keep their status private. When the Princess told me it was time for her baby a few weeks later, and she wanted me to participate, I begged off, saying I had heard there was measles at her home and I did not wish to suffer my child with the disease."

"If I understand you correctly, my good woman, are you saying that Princess Caroline told you she was pregnant before you conceived, but did not deliver her child until after you delivered yours?"

"Not exactly, Your Honour. I cannot vouch for the birth of the child the Princess showed me later. I did not see or witness the birth."

"I see. Do you have an opinion as to who might be the father of this mysterious child, Lady Douglas?"

"That would be right hard to determine, Your Honour," she replied, "seeing as to the number of gentleman callers the Princess has."

Instantaneous laughter permeated the room.

"I mean to say the Princess was rarely in a dearth of male companionship."

The laughter spiked again and the men and women turned to each other.

"What I meant to say was Caroline was always entertaining male companions."

The crowd erupted in laughter, with some men slapping their laps.

"No, you've got it all wrong! The Princess..."

"Thank you, Lady Douglas. Your testimony was most helpful. Please stand down."

"Yes, Your honour."

"We now wish to call Mr. Thomas Stikeman."

The short, stocky, well-dressed, well-mannered gentleman rose and took the seat vacated by Lady Douglas.

The Lord Chief Justice began the inquiry, "Please explain your position with Her Royal Highness, Princess Caroline."

"Yes, of course M'Lord," he began, a bit nervous at having to answer questions that might implicate his charge. "I am Page to Her Highness and have been ever since her arrival to England some ten years ago."

"And being Page to the Princess, you have access to Her Highness constantly?"

"Oh yes, M'Lord. No man is closer to the Princess what hasn't bedded her."

The crowd chuckled.

"Therefore, if the Princess was with child, you would undoubtedly know of her condition?"

"Not so much, M'Lord. The Princess gains weight and loses weight from time to time, and when she is plumper, I imagine one could get the idea that she was with child. She hasn't looked much different from when she was carrying the Princess Charlotte."

"I see, and in your opinion, were there any men in her life, other than the Prince, who could have caused her to be with child?"

"Well, M'Lord, the Princess is quite popular with the gentlemen," a few people laughed at this, "and she had two particular callers who spent more time with her than others, but..."

"And who would those two gentlemen be, Mr. Stikeman?" The Page looked about the room as if to seek counsel. "I shall remind you that you are under the King's command and must answer all questions put before you with openness and honesty, Mr. Stikeman."

"Ummm, then that would be Sir Sidney Smith and Captain Manby, when his ship, the *Africaine*, was in port, M'Lord."

"Thank you, Mr. Stikeman. And in your opinion, and knowledge of Her Highness, do you believe that either of these two frequent gentleman callers could be the father of such a child, if Princess Caroline conceived in 1802?"

"No, M'Lord, not at all."

Lord Law stared hard at the deponent. "And what leads you to this certainty, sir?"

"Well, M'Lord, the father is a neighbour of mine, a dock worker named William Austin."

The Chief Justice interrupted, "Are you suggesting the Princess Caroline has borne a child with a common dock hand!?"

"Not at all, M'Lord!" the page gasped. "Heaven forfend such an act. Austin's wife Sophia is the mother. Mr. Austin approached me when he heard the Princess was looking to have a child. He told me he could get one for me. They could no longer afford another mouth to feed after the redundancies due to The Peace. I figured it would be better to have an infant from someone we know, rather than a stranger. The baby was born in Brownlow Street. He brought the child a few days later and I snuck it into the Princess's chambers. She named him William, Willikin, she calls him. I have heard Her Highness tell people that it is her child, but I know the truth, M'Lord, and have kept my mouth shut–until just now that is."

"An interesting tale, Mr. Stikeman, to be sure. And you are confident this child is not a result of the Prince and Princess?"

"With certainty, M'Lord."

"And to the best of your ability, are you aware of any criminal intercourse or improper familiarity on the part of Her Highness, the Princess of Wales?"

"Not at all, M'Lord. The most improper conduct I have ever observed Her Highness engage in is kissing a gentleman, but in the manner of two friends, two very close friends."

"I see. And was that Sir Sidney or Captain Manby?"

"Sir Sidney, M'Lord, but the Princess is vivacious and frequently familiar with gentlemen."

"So we are to believe. Thank you, Mr. Stikeman. That is all."

"Yes, M'Lord," and he hobbled off.

Lord Law continued, "Next we would like to call up Miss Betty Townley."

Britain's Glory

The somewhat disheveled working girl made her way to the chair. She had put her scattered mousy brown hair up in a bun, but wisps escaped and bounced as she walked.

"Yes, Yer Lordship?" she inquired, displaying a few brown teeth.

"Please sit, Miss Townley," and he indicated the seat.

"Thankin' Yer Lordship," and she daintily positioned herself.

"Now, Miss Townley, what is your position in the Royal household?"

"I, meself, ha' been in the employ of the Princess Caroline some sixteen years of me life, both at the Carlton and the Montague 'ouses as laundry lady, Yer Lordship."

"I see. And over the years, you have personally handled the bedsheets of Her Highness?"

"Oh, yes, Yer Lordship. They are of the finest Damask napkin, they are!"

"Of course, and from time to time have you noticed anything that might lead one to believe that the Princess had engaged in activities unbecoming a princess?"

Betty looked around the room sheepishly, "Am I at liberty to speak frank-like, Yer Lordship? I do not wish to diminish the character of Her Highness, but I have been diein' to tell someone."

"Miss Townley, your candid testimony is paramount to the consummation of this inquiry."

"Beg pardon, Yer Lordship?"

"Feel free to speak your mind, madam," he responded, eyes toward the ceiling.

"Right, Yer Lordship. It may not be for someone as lowly as meself to say, but from the nasty bits we see from time to time on the linens, I would have to say the Princess is fairly fond o' fuckin'."

The entire room broke into laughter.

Charlotte: The People's Princess

"Silence!" yelled the Lord Chief Justice, "Order! Order!"

When the uproar subsided, Betty asked, "I am fearfully sorry, Yer Lordship, did I say somethin' wrong?"

"No, Miss Townley, you spoke your truth, exactly what was asked of you. It is just that these people are not used to hearing it in such a... direct fashion, shall we say."

"Begging' Yer Lordship's pardon, I know I hain't as educated as the rest of you lot," she waved a hand at the crowd, "but I do an honest day's work for meagre wages, and that is enow for the likes o' me."

"And we appreciate your service, madam." He exhaled heavily before continuing, "Despite the condition of the bedsheets, have you ever personally observed the Princess engaging in criminal sexual intercourse?"

"I hain't never seen 'er 'ighness engaged in any sexual intercourse, criminal nor otherwise."

A few people chuckled, and Lord Law held up his hand to quiet the crowd. "Miss Townley, during the time period between the Summer of 1802 and a year later, when the Austin child first appeared at the residence of the Princess, were there any unusual episodes regarding Her Highness's bedclothes?"

"Begging' Yer Lordship's pardon again, I find 'er 'ighness's bedclothes unusual all the time."

Once more the crowd giggled and the Lord Chief Justice held up his hand. "I mean to ask if there were any instances far outside what you would normally expect of Her Highness's bedclothes."

Betty put her finger to her forehead as if in great thought, "1802... Summertime... Yeah! Indeed there was somethin' very strange in the Damask there was!"

"Pray enlighten us, madam."

"Of course, Yer Lordship," and she squirmed about in the chair, getting into a more preferred position, "One mornin' in August–or it might ha' been September or October, I can't rightly remember–I was sent into 'er 'ighness's chamber to collect the soiled sheets. To my surprise, as you can well imagine, the Damask was all bloody and messy! At first I thought the Princess might have offed someone durin' the night, but then I realised it reminded me of when I meself had lost a child midway through the pregnancy it did. Wot you might be callin' a miscarriage. The blood, the clots, it was a pretty mess it was! When I told the chamberlady about what I had found, she said the Princess had been bled with leeches the day before and that's where all the bloody mess came from."

Lord Law paused in reflection, "And is it of your opinion Miss Townley, that the blood came from the bleeding?"

"I hain't no bleedin' surgeon, Yer Lordship! If you are after gettin' some medical advice, might I suggest you inquire of Mr. Edmeades, the gentleman wot preformed the bloody bleedin'. I accepted wot I was told as fact. It hain't me place to judge 'er 'ighness!"

4 November 1817, Claremont House, Surrey
Night

"Leo, wake up." The Prince had fallen asleep sitting on the floor, his back to the wall of the room where his wife lay attempting to deliver their first child.

"Is there news?" Leopold rubbed at his eyes.

"Not exactly. The contractions have diminished, the Princess has fallen asleep and our visitors have retired for the night. Perhaps you should get some rest as well, Leo."

"Stockmar," the Prince placed his palms on the floor, "it has been 24 hours since the beginning of the contractions."

"Yes."

"Is that usual?"

"Deliveries are unique beings. Each is different. Some mothers deliver quickly, others do not." He glanced down to assess the Prince's mood. "Charlotte is a strong woman with a very strong will. Leave her to determine the proper timing."

"I suppose you know best. You always do." He struggled to stand due to extreme exhaustion.

"Shall I have your dinner sent up?"

"Yes, please. And have some extra sherry on the tray, thank you."

"Of course, Your Highness. Get some sleep, Leo. Tomorrow shall also be challenging."

Britain's Glory

Parliament Building

6 February 1811, House of Parliament, Winchester
Late morning

Originally built during the Middle Ages, recently remodeled, the House of Parliament stands squarely on the north bank of the River Thames. In expansive Westminster Hall, the most powerful men in the British government, with the exception of the reigning monarch, met to discuss a delicate matter of state.

The pale and balding George Spencer of Percival, now Prime Minister, took a sip of sherry and addressed the assembled Privy Council and Prince George from the Speaker's stand at the front of the long hall, "By reason of His Majesty's on-going health issues," coughing and muttering from the crowd interrupted him briefly, "ongoing declining health, the Parliament has approved George, Prince of Wales, to serve as Regent during his father's infirmity."

Some of the Members of Parliament glanced at each other. A few nodded, one stood at the back of the hall glancing out the window.

At this the Prince attempted to raise his bloated carcass to bow, but could not muster the strength, and he simply waved to the gentlemen around the room. The Tory onlookers merely said "Hear, hear" blandly and the Whigs gave a few lackluster huzzahs.

"However," the Prime Minister interrupted, "we have set out a listing of restrictions upon His Highness's regency..."

"Not permanent, I presume," blurted out the Prince, who appeared slightly inebriated.

"These restrictions are to remain in place for a period of one year, after which, if the King has not returned to full health, the Prince Regent will be free and unrestricted to rule as He sees fit."

"Hear, hear!" the Prince shouted. "Hear, hear!"

Charlotte: The People's Princess

The Prime Minister raised his hand, "The Prince Regent shall not create peers nor award offices nor pensions. Her Royal Highness, the Queen shall be responsible for the care of the King, and the King's private property shall be looked after by a panel of trustees."

"Look! It's Princess Charlotte!" the man standing at the rear screamed and pointed out the window. All heads, save the Prince, turned to catch a glimpse of the resplendent young woman riding past. Her riding clothes accentuated the newly-developed curves of her adolescent body. The horse's breath turned to rising steam in the brisk February air. As she rode off, the onlookers started to glance again at the puffy, libidinous, overextended creature they just appointed to lead the nation. A few sighs could be heard, some of admiration for the Princess, some of disgust at the Prince.

"She's turned and approaches again!" another onlooker announced as the Members of Parliament once again shifted their singular gaze to the young woman who would be Queen when the two hated and despised Georges expired.

"What a bloody nuisance!" the Prince bellowed. "This is to be my ceremony, not my daughter's. Gentlemen, I pray we return to the business at hand." George's anger toward Charlotte's intentional distraction ruffled his molting feathers.

"Yes, of course, Your Highness," the Prime Minister intoned. "Does the Prince Regent wish to address the assemblage?"

"I'm betting he does," mumbled one of the gentlemen. "I would like to imagine that Prinny is about to call for elections, send the Tories packing and install a Whig government."

"Yes, indeed, Mr. Prime Minister, We would like to address the assemblage."

As the overplump Prince struggled to stand, the progressive Whig members of Parliament shook hands and slapped each other on the back. "All of our hard work and support of the Prince is about to pay off," said one MP.

"Thank you all for your support during this difficult time for our Royal Family," grumbles of discontent bubbled through the crowd. Most of the nation had become fed up with the Hanover Family's ill-mannered behaviors, sex scandals and abuse of the Royal Treasury. "In deference to my father, the King, We shall leave all of the Government as it stands. Should he return to his senses and the throne, We do not wish for His Majesty to find His reign and ministers disrupted or changed."

Whigs inhaled as one, having expected the Prince to support them as they had supported him. The conservative Tories, happy to retain their control of Parliament, nodded ascent.

One of the Whig MPs said to another in a hushed tone, "I can only imagine the sweet whisperings of George's Tory whore directly into his pudgy ear could have brought about this result."

5 November 1817, Claremont House, Surrey
Early morning

Baron Stockmar cautiously opened the door to the Prince's bedroom and peeked in. A few streams of sunlight dotted the carpet and walls. Leopold sat up in his bed.

"Well, my dear Stockmar, how do we fare on this new day?"

"Good morning to you, Leo." He entered the chamber and approached the Prince. "The Princess sleeps still. Do you wish to call?"

"Yes, I think I should. A bit of encouragement might be just what she needs." He shuffled out of the bed clothes and stood.

The Baron briefly observed Leopold's appearance. "Seems like you slept well. Feeling better?"

Charlotte: The People's Princess

"A bit, a bit." He reached for his housecoat and put it on. "A new day, a new start. By day's end I shall be a proud father. Yes?"

"Of course, Leo, of course."

They walked together to Charlotte's chamber.

Royal Opera House

22 February 1812, Royal Opera House, Covent Garden, London
Evening

As Prince George and his fellowship proceeded toward the Royal Box, his voice could be heard throughout the theatre. "I have no idea why the fucking Whigs are so enraged. I have offered them a bloody coalition, which is precisely what they have been after. My father's Tories will most assuredly remain in power as long as I sit as Regent, their party being the most in line with the Royal wishes." He and his retinue had just finished a lavish roast beef dinner, replete with many bottles of port and sherry.

Whig members in the audience plugged their ears or pinched their noses. Foremost among them the bald but stately Earl Charles Grey, leader of the loyal Whig opposition, sitting in the box directly across. Even Princess Charlotte, who had to sit next to her father, seemed visibly annoyed at the Prince's rantings. After all, this was her first night at the opera and, at 16 years of age, she imagined she would be the centre of attention, not the hated old man who had tried to keep her out of sight and locked up with her bitter old maiden aunts for most of her life. Earlier in the evening she had to endure the tiresome dinner with her obnoxious father and the doting old men who surrounded him waiting for a royal crumb to fall their way. It was bad enough that she had to wear a moth-eaten gown handed down from her Aunt Mary.

George pointed toward Lord Grey, "What in bloody hell do those faggots want from us? Perhaps We should start calling them 'Whiggots'!" he roared. To the empty stage he commanded, "Start the bloody show already! Bring out the bird with the ample bosom!" chuckling and gesticulating drunkenly.

At this, Charlotte stood to leave with tears welling up. She remembered how the Whigs supported her father against the Tories, who initially opposed him, time after time. As a child she was determined to pledge herself to the Whigs and their proposed reforms, bringing Britain solidly into the modern realm of the 19th Century.

However, when the audience caught sight of her starting to leave, they clapped wildly. "Charlotte, don't go!" someone shouted. "Princess, please stay!" yelled another. A chant of "Stay, please stay" soon reverberated around the theatre.

Not knowing what to do, she began waving to the crowd, as she had done at the few public appearances her over-controlling father had allowed her to make. Seeing the Princess's response, the crowd got even louder and more desirous of her attention.

Prince George turned redder, "I don't know what you're attempting to do, you self-willed little wench, but you won't be seeing the light of day much after this grand performance!" Charlotte pretended not to hear her father and continued to make love with the audience. He grabbed her wrist, "Enough! You whore mongrel bitch of a child! How dare you receive applause like that in my presence. They should be cheering their Prince Regent and not you, missie! You cunt daughter of a gas-sucking whore of a mother!"

Not liking her father's behavior or speech, Princess Charlotte broke free of his grasp and turned directly toward Earl Grey, the Prince's current political arch-enemy, smiled and blew kisses to him. The crowd went wild with delight, whooping and chanting her name, much to her father's increasing disgust. With a grand flourish, she kissed her hand and held it out in Earl Grey's direction. As the ovation subsided, she turned to her father, smiled knowingly at him, and then left promptly.

5 November 1817, Claremont House, Surrey
Morning

> "The labour of her Royal Highness the Princess Charlotte has within the last three or four hours considerably advanced, and will, it is hoped, within a few hours be happily completed." – Progress report from Sir Richard Croft to the Prince Regent

As Prince Leopold started to enter the confinement chamber, he could see his dear Charlotte with a look of horror on her face. Eyes wide open mouth aghast, she was looking at someone or something just out of sight. A fetid smell permeated the room, sweat in the bedclothes blended with urine. He remained near the door, where she could not see him.

Britain's Glory

"Get that bloody torture device out of my sight!" Sir Richard Croft ordered. One of the attendant physicians held a metal device that resembled two ladles screwed together like scissors.

"Begging pardon, Sir Richard, but if the Princess is too weak to deliver the child on her own, we may need to assist the birthing." The younger doctor attempted to reason with the accoucher.

"No, I say. No!"

"But Sir Richard, this is the most modern Chamberlen device for difficult births such as this." A bit of light from the bedside lamp reflected off the shiny metallic surface, giving the appearance of sparks.

"No royal child shall be yanked from its mother's womb by a medieval inquisitor's tool under my supervision! The birth must be ordained and natural, not at man's behest." Croft waved his hands about as if he were sermonising.

"Of course, Sir Richard. I suppose that a Caesar-style incision is also out of the question."

"Indubitably!" Croft expelled. "Ordained and natural!"

Prince Leopold stepped backward out of the chamber making as little noise as possible.

Windsor Castle

August 1812, Prince Regent's Chambers, Royal Lodge, Windsor
Early afternoon

"Lord Liverpool, We appreciate your making the hasty trip up from London," Prince George stated, ushering the new Prime Minister into the modest drawing room. While not as grandiose and sumptuous as Carlton House in London or as radiant and ornate as the Royal Pavilion at Brighton, the recently-acquired Royal Lodge was stately and conservative, at least for now.

"Naturally. I trust Your Highness would not have called me up without an important matter confronting the nation," replied Richard Jenkinson, Earl of Liverpool, now serving as Prime Minister. He was middle-aged and greying, still tall but not as dashing as in his youth.

"Of course, but let Us first express Our appreciation for your standing for this office after the untimely death of Lord Perceval." The previous Prime Minister had been shot at point blank range by a disgruntled constituent in May just outside the Houses of Parliament. Prince George selected Jenkinson as the replacement and muscled the appointment through, even with vigorous opposition to having yet another Tory leader.

"Thank you, Your Highness, I shall endeavor to serve crown and country with honour." He looked upon George's behemoth belly and thought of the recent popular poem referring to him as "The Prince of Whales" and considered perhaps the epithet may not have gone far enough.

"We have no doubt of that, Lord Liverpool. Now to the matters at hand." The Prince fished a fig from the bowl on the table beside him and slurped it like an oyster. "We wish to discuss the despicable behavior of Princess Charlotte."

"Beg pardon, Your Highness?"

The Prince looked down his bulbous nose at Jenkinson, "We are not tolerating the Princess's expression of free will. She has disgraced Us in public, written libelous letters suggesting

We treat her badly, and she disobeys direct orders from the Prince Regent."

Liverpool's eyes widened in disbelief, "And that is the pressing business you summoned me away from Winchester to address? With all due respect, Your Highness, I am dealing with two concurrent military engagements on two continents, declining revenues, growing unrest, and I hardly think this matter rises to the level of urgency to which you have assigned it." He turned to leave.

Prince George slapped his flabby hand on the table, "Mr. Prime Minister, must We remind you that it has been over a year since Our installation as Prince Regent and We are now at liberty to rule the nation without restriction. If We decide this matter is of national importance, it is of national importance."

"Yes, of course, Your Highness," Liverpool turned back, lowered his eyes and quickly reviewed options in his mind. He looked up again, with his nose pointed slightly higher, "How may I assist you?"

"The Princess needs to learn her place. If she is to serve as Queen in the future, she must marry before it is too late. Her taste in male companionship does not meet with Our approval. My agents tell me she has fraternised openly with one military officer and clandestinely met with another. They have observed her mother, the Princess of Wales" and at the mention of Wales, Liverpool had to fight back the giggles "facilitating these meetings, much to Our dismay."

Liverpool thought about his encounters with the youthful Princess, recalling her tales of being kept out of public view by the Prince, then spoke, "Perhaps young Charlotte is still sour about not being invited to your accession ball. It was quite the topic of conversation that evening and for the next few weeks." He observed George posing as if considering the invasion of France. "The public craves your daughter's attention and continues to wonder as to her whereabouts. Some fear you wish to keep her locked away, removed from her loyal subjects, secreted for some self-serving purpose, Your Highness."

Charlotte: The People's Princess

"Mr. Prime Minister," puffed the Prince, "We shall raise the Princess as We see fit. As to your inquisitive innuendos, the Princess needed to attend her grandmother, the Queen, that evening and would not have been able to be present."

"Again, I must ask: how may I assist you?" Jenkinson inquired, trying to maintain his calm while thinking of the more difficult situations awaiting him back in London.

"We are attempting to negotiate a good marriage for the Princess. The Hereditary Prince William of Orange is Our first choice, for political advantage. However, once married, the Princess shall be remaining in Holland most of the time."

Jenkinson could see at once that the Prince Regent was merely attempting to remove his daughter from the public attention he felt should be his. "Your Highness, these days, most young women make their own choice of husband."

"My agents also inform me the Princess has been reading that blasphemous Jane Austen." He waved his hand as if dismissing a servant. "Filling the heads of our young women with thoughts of independence will be the ruin of this nation. In addition, her friend, Miss Elphinstone, also encourages defiance in Charlotte. My daughter will marry who I tell her to marry and that is that!"

"I believe it is 'whom,' Your Highness. 'Whom I tell her to marry.'"

Prince George stared at the Prime Minister intently, "Are you a Member of Parliament or the Grammar Master, sir? I beg of you to remember your place here."

"I am sorry that you have brought me all the way out here merely to discuss parental matters. Seeing that I have yet to produce issue, I fear that I will be of little assistance in this situation. Pray excuse me as I must return to London directly." He turned to leave and stopped, "I bid you good day, Your Highness," and then continued out of the chamber.

"Wait!" George roared, "We have not yet dismissed you!"

♦ 45 ♦

Britain's Glory

The Prime Minister shouted from the hallway, "I bid you good day, Your Highness."

"Blast!" shouted the Prince as he grasped empty air with his flabby fist.

5 November 1817, Claremont House, Surrey
Late morning

Prince Leopold stood by the chaise grasping the hand of his wife tenderly. He gazed at Charlotte, feeling her anguish and shame.

She opened her mouth to speak, but he placed his finger gently on her lips, "Save your strength, my love. It shan't be much longer."

She smiled weakly and turned her head away.

"Croft!" beckoned Leopold, "what can we do?"

"Wait, Your Highness, merely wait," Sir Richard responded and he went back to reading his book.

The Prince stroked Charlotte's hand with his sweat-moistened palm. "We have been waiting a long time for this, *meine Schatze*, what are a few more moments?"

Charlotte glared at him with one eye slightly closed.

"Hours?" he suggested.

She attempted to pull her hand away, but Leopold held tightly. "Days, if necessary." He smiled and winked at her reassuringly. "I will not leave your side, even if it takes a week to deliver our child."

Charlotte smiled back and grasped his hand a bit tighter.

House of Lords

2 December 1812, House of Lords, Parliament Building, Westminster, London
Late morning

Princess Charlotte sat on the Woolsack (usually the seat of the Lord Speaker) in front of the throne, looking about the great hall for sight of people she knew. Glad to be out in public, even directly under the scrutinising eye of her father, who struggled to climb the steps to deliver his speech opening Parliament.

Earlier in the day, the Yeomen of the Guard searched the rooms below. In 1605, a group of disgruntled Catholics attempted to blow up the building to kill the Protestant King James I. Merely a formality now, the cellars are routinely searched if the Monarch is to address Parliament.

She caught the eye of Earl Grey and waved in his direction. Erskine and Jersey also received recognition. Lord Liverpool was nowhere to be found. The Princess had not yet received education regarding the British government's particulars, and it is customary for the sitting Prime Minister to be locked in the Palace while the Monarch is in Parliament, thus assuring the safe return of the Monarch. Purely ceremonial, the practice continued ever onward in perpetuity, as did most stale traditions.

The carriage ride from the palace had been most enjoyable. People cheered and called out her name, hoping to catch a glimpse of the unconventional Princess they admired so. Unfortunately, she could not wave to the crowd because the cramped compartment did not allow for such things.

She had ridden with her maiden aunts, Sophie and Mary. In some aspects, Charlotte felt a rivalry with her Aunt Mary, the youngest of her father's sisters and the most attractive woman of her 11 aunts and uncles. Not much older than Princess Charlotte, Mary probably imagined it should be she, and not her starstruck niece, who should be receiving of the public's attention and affection. She should have the pick of handsome Continental Princes looking to join with Britain's royal line, not some young upstart with very few social graces. But somehow the people loved Charlotte more than any of the rest of the Hanovers. Perhaps it was her fresh approach, her ability to connect with the crowd or maybe because she was directly in line for the most powerful throne in the world, and Britons hoped she would restore the elegance and glory her extended family had destroyed.

Prince George raised his arm to signal the beginning of the proceedings. The Gentleman Usher strode from the back of the room to the front near Charlotte.

"Mr. Speaker, The King commends this honourable House," the Usher bowed to the assembled Members of Parliament, "to attend His Majesty."

As the Prince Regent prepared to make his remarks, Charlotte continued to gaze around, waving to the assembled members and Lords. Her father looked down at her briefly, as if admonishing her. She ignored his gesture, turned her back to him and continued to connect with the Whig ministers who adored her every action.

The Prince Regent began, "My Lords and Members of the House of Commons, I pray that the blessing of the Almighty may rest upon your counsels." A few Members applauded quietly. Many continued their personal conversations, taking little notice of the Prince's speech.

As her father rambled on about estimates for public services, agendas for the coming year and other unintelligible prattle, Charlotte maintained an enigmatic smile and studied the faces of the men she would one day have sway over, trying to remember their names.

5 November 1817, Claremont House, Surrey
Afternoon

Prince Leopold paced the short hallway outside Charlotte's chamber. The physicians had asked him to leave the room so that his wife could relax. As much as he hated leaving her side, knowing that his friend Stockmar was there made it a bit easier. He glanced down to examine the runner carpet for signs of wear due to his walking back and forth over the same path.

His thoughts strayed to happier times when he and the Princess lived in London, seeing plays, dining with friends and family, socialising with other European dignitaries. After the baby was grown a bit, he was certain they would return to their bourgeois lifestyle that he missed so dearly. For now, the Prince would have to content himself playing lord of the manor in the countryside. So provincial compared to life in a large city.

The door to the chamber opened and roused him from his thoughts. Baron Stockmar poked his head through the opening.

"Leo! Come quickly! The contractions are starting up again. Charlotte needs you!"

The Prince dashed into his wife's room.

Britain's Glory

Sandhurst Academy

12 August 1813, Sandhurst Military Academy, Berkshire
Evening

The Royal Military College had recently moved its operations to Sandhurst in Berkshire. Tonight marked the official opening of the new Army Officer Training campus.

The day had consisted of dedication ceremonies, including a consecration by Reverend Dr. Fisher, the Great UP. Prince George also used the occasion to host his birthday festivities. Although turning 51, he looked in the mirror and saw 25.

In addition, it was to be the first meeting of the prospective suitors, the Hereditary Prince to the throne of Holland and Britain's Princess of Wales. Charlotte attended the gala, as ordered by her father to meet her assigned fiancé for the first time, wearing the finest things her personal dresser, Louise Louis, could find. A miniature portrait of the Princess had been sent to Prince William, who found Charlotte's looks acceptable. Charlotte had no idea what her potential fiancé looked like. All she knew was that her future husband lived in England most of his life while his family was in exile. Now that the royal family prepared to return home to Holland, they wanted a bride for their heir apparent.

Charlotte: The People's Princess

She entered the large room, the academy mess hall decorated with royal panache for this occasion, and greeted other guests who were thrilled to meet the Princess in person. She charmed them with her childish exuberance, and they pressed to learn more about the woman who would one day be their Queen. Her father had kept her public appearances to a minimum, preferring Charlotte to stay out of the general eye for his own selfish reasons. The Prince Regent only requested his daughter's presence this evening to introduce her to the man he wanted her to marry. Although the main function of the evening was to inaugurate the academy, it was still His birthday festival.

Prince George was well known for his lavish parties, all at the citizens' expense, and this was no exception. Roast pigs, geese and venison waited to be carved and served. Each table had a large loaf of fresh bread and two carafes of wine, red and white. A room full of the British elite in their finery, titled gentlemen and their wives, and expensive decorative appointments–all part of an evening with the Prince of Wales.

Across the room Charlotte could see her father tossing back glass after glass of fortified spirits with his usual entourage around the central dining table and one gangly young fellow whom she found rather plain. Prince George laughed loudly, and his mates followed suit. The young Prince William of Orange, also known to his friends as "Slim Willy," then burst into giggles as well. After a half hour, the constantly refilled bottles circled the table a few more times and Frederick, the Duke of York, fell over backwards in his chair, banging his head on a wine cooler. He then tried to pull himself up by grabbing the tablecloth, and only succeeded in pulling the entire contents of the table down upon him. More laughter ensued.

One by one the drunken lot began some silly schooldays drinking game and removed their clothing piece by piece. Within minutes, the Prince Regent could no longer manage to remain in his chair and he slid silently under the table, followed in sequence by His Highness's advisors and allies. As each man fell to the floor, the group whooped in hilarity.

Britain's Glory

The last person to slip from view was Charlotte's intended, William, Hereditary Prince of Orange.

Seeing that this was not the best opportunity to have a first meeting with the man her father wanted her to marry, Charlotte excused herself and left.

5 November 1817, Claremont House, Surrey
Late afternoon

Prince Leopold sat holding his dozing wife's hand. The contractions had ceased after about an hour. He could sense the relief Charlotte felt from both having the birth commence and also from having it pause. With no nourishment, the Princess lacked the energy to deliver a child properly.

Henry Addington, the Home Secretary, slowly opened the door from the darkened hallway. Hearing no objection, he poked his head through the opening to observe the situation.

Croft sat across the room nibbling on an apple slice and sipping a glass of port sherry.

"Sir Richard," Addington broke the silence, "may I enquire into the progress of your patient?"

The accoucheur looked up at the visitor, sniffed the air with a wince and blinked. "I believe you read my dispatch of earlier today, Mr. Secretary?"

"Yes, I did, Sir Richard," Addington responded, slightly offended at the haughty tone of the physician, "however, the Archbishop and I must return to London soon. Your communiqué indicated an approximate delivery for the early afternoon."

Charlotte: The People's Princess

"If the Princess," Croft pointed at Charlotte with an apple slice, "had followed my recommendations all along, there may not have been such delay." He took a bite of the slice. "As it is, I can only estimate with broad certainty, Mr. Secretary."

Addington arched one eyebrow and turned to Prince Leopold, who shrugged. He then backed out of the room and closed the door as Sir Richard popped the rest of the apple slice into his mouth.

11 December 1813, Warwick House, London
Evening

The Prince Regent, holding an apple, waddled into the darkened sitting room where his daughter sat practicing piano by candlelight. As soon as she saw her father, she abruptly stopped playing and started to rise.

"Charlotte!" bellowed the Prince Regent, "Stay where you are!" He pointed his sausage finger at her where she stood. "Sit down, wench." He took a large bite from the apple.

Once Charlotte sat back down, her father made his way to a chaise that could handle his bulk. Persistent gout caused him to move even slower than before. He exhaled heavily upon settling and then turned to face his daughter.

"We shall speak, and you shall listen."

She closed her eyes, wishing she could close her ears as well.

"As of late, We have noticed a trend in your manner, a growing disrespectful and unappreciative attitude, obvious to all. Prithee remember the society ball We managed for you at Oatlands." The Princess cocked her head as in disbelief. "Yes, that Highland Flurry nonsense you made Us dance caused a turned ankle that landed Us in bed, unable to walk, clouded with laudanum for a month. A month! And a month which brought the wheels of government to a halt because We could not conduct its regular business from a strange bed in Oatlands! Our enemies even put forth the idea that We were beginning to succumb to your grandfather's illness."

His daughter stifled a laugh.

George narrowed his eyes at her and raised an eyebrow. "Earlier this year–sometime in March–you made quite a scene with your porcine mother in Piccadilly. Carriage races, public hugging through the windows and an extended interview with her while blocking the normal flow of vehicles. You might as well have ordered the porters to summon quenching pints." He bulged his eyes at her. "Did you think such news would manage to avoid Our ears? Do you not remember you have been forbidden to have any contact with that whore!"

The Princess stared at her father menacingly.

"When you were in cradle, it was not that sack of flab who took care of you. *We* stood by you in your early days, watching over your safety, ensuring your care. It is to *Us* you owe your allegiance, not that adipose sow!" He pointed in a direction vaguely toward northwest.

Charlotte slowly shook her head in disbelief.

"Certain papers have been delivered to you through the Duchess of Leeds demonstrating the unbecoming behavior of your mother, the Princess of Wales, as chronicled in the Delicate Investigation before the Prime Minister." The Prince referred to the episode of 1806, seven years prior, when then Prime Minister William Grenville and other officials questioned associates and staff of Charlotte's mother in an attempt to give Prince George reason to end his unpleasant marriage. The tribunal found no evidence of wrongdoing on the part of Princess Caroline.

"We have even attempted to make amends by gifting you the royal sapphire from the recently recovered crown of Charles the First." He squinted and glanced at the ovoid gem dangling between his daughter's ample breasts and then bit off another chunk of apple.

The Princess touched the ancestor's stone and prayed her fate would not be the same as his.

"Furthermore," he said between chews, "We are most distressed at your behavior concerning the Prince of Orange. A marriage between the two of you shall take place because he is the only person We approve."

Charlotte's head fell so that her chin touched her bosom.

"One of Our ministers has reported that you have consistently refused to consider such an arrangement. It has also come to Our attention that you have publicly declared you might not marry anyone."

Charlotte opened her mouth, but before she could utter a sound, her father roared, "Silence! You shall not speak! Only We shall speak in this interview."

She closed her mouth and turned her head away.

"You may try to turn aside, but you shall hear all We have to say."

Charlotte grimaced.

"Earlier this year you petitioned to quit your governess and employ a lady of the bedchamber instead. And your choice, Admiral Elphinstone's daughter, Miss Mercer–your bosom companion–is supremely unfit for this delicate position. Such impertinence was answered with unanimity of the Prince Regent, the Queen, and the Lord Chancellor. We all agreed you were too young to be out from under the management of a governess, especially given your propensity to disobey direct orders, appear in public without Our permission, and live under the illusion that you are some kind of independent woman of the world. Our dearest daughter, you shall never–NEVER–be independent. Until you are married, you are under Our direct control. After marriage you shall submit to your husband, the unlucky sod. And, should the unfortunate day arrive when you take the throne of this great nation, you will thenceforth be beholden to it, as We are now discovering. The inopportune circumstances of your birth as the heir to the throne have dictated your future." He pointed at her for effect. "The sooner you accept your pre-ordained fate, the sooner we shall all get along better. Some days I doubt whether you are even Our child." Another bite of apple.

The Princess squirmed in the chair and dropped her hands to her lap.

Her father chewed noisily and continued, "It has also been decided that you shall not have further uncensored interaction with your disgusting mother. All communications shall be read before transmittal, and every call will be chaperoned." He paused to swallow. "It has come to Our attention she is attempting to use you as a pawn in her every scheme to curry favour and We do not wish Our daughter to be mistreated as such. Do you understand?"

Charlotte nodded ever so slightly.

"Excellent! Further, since the August celebration, you have managed to avoid every event at which Prince William has attended in hopes of meeting you. He subsequently returned to the Continent and We employed Lady Osborne to surveil you. While you attempted to keep her from understanding you by speaking in foreign tongues with your friend Miss Elphinstone and locking her in the necessary, she has given me a full report of your activities."

The Princess snapped to face her father with surprise.

"Yes," the Prince Regent continued, "and that is why We sent Sir Henry to you in an attempt to educate you on the charms of Prince William. And after over an hour of his instruction, you told him you favoured the Duke of Gloucester, who is out of the question, as We am sure you well know."

Again, she turned her head away.

"It is Our desire to keep Holland affixed to this island as tightly as possible. There is even a Russian order of knighthood awaiting you, St. Catherine, We believe, when you become betrothed, and it is widely known how much you favour Russia."

Charlotte puffed air through her lips.

"Our dear daughter, William may be plain, excessively slender and have nasty dentition, but Gloucester is bloody ugly! A veritable slice of cheese. You had to have been under the constant influence of alcoholic spirits to find any charm in that turd of a man!"

Charlotte stared at her father through narrow eye slits, her controlled anger keeping the lids from touching.

"And if Our sources are correct, he has a pining for Our sister, your aunt, Mary. We fear it is just another foolish ruse of yours to deflect the observation of your true feelings. There is chatter that you may have your eye on some other dandy, such as Devonshire."

At that suggestion, she looked away yet again.

"Besides, We are aware of what transpired in Windsor Park with your Captain Hesse. Your obnoxious mother may have employed him to convey correspondence, but he is beneath your station and unsuitable as a potential husband. You will terminate your communications with him immediately. If it were not for Our clemency, We would lock you up for life!"

Charlotte tensed all her muscles.

"Depend upon it, as long as We live you shall never have an establishment, unless you marry." He bit the last edible part of the apple.

The Princess inhaled and exhaled audibly while her father gnashed his teeth.

"You are the most eligible young woman on the planet, and there are princes a-plenty waiting to swoop you off to lands unknown. Now, We are aware that you have read the suggestive works of Miss Jane Austen and her insistence that women should have the right to choose their own husband. Granted, this is a new Century, and traditions shall most likely change, but you are not the average girl living in your parents' country home. You are on queue for the throne of Great Britain, and you shall marry only with the Monarch's express consent."

Charlotte exhaled heavily through her nose.

"You may have noticed," her father droned on, "as of late We have been more attentive to Your Highness. During this past week We have made an effort to be more... courteous and pleasant." To which the Princess rolled her eyes in contempt. "And now We expect your cooperation in return."

Making an effort, Charlotte studied the Prince Regent's bloated face for a clue.

"A portrait of Prince William of Orange has been placed in your chamber so that you may study it and become more accustomed to his visage. Now that he is returned from the Continent following the conclusion of the unpleasantness from that little French fellow, you are expected to attend tomorrow evening's dinner at Carlton. No excuses. *Comprenez-vous, chère fille?*"

When the Princess did not respond, Prince George snorted. "Nodding your head will be sufficient." After a few seconds he commanded, "Nod your fucking head, bitch!" He struggled to stand.

Princess Charlotte slowly moved her head up and down. "God damn you, Charlotte, you are verily Our daughter." He placed the apple core on the dark wooden stand next to the chaise as he waddled away.

5 November 1817, Claremont House, Surrey
Late afternoon

Leopold had serious concerns regarding Charlotte's health. Her face was grey, her pulse extremely weak, her hair damp and matted. He wanted to smack the side of Croft's face in hopes of making the bastard realise how poorly he was taking care of the Princess. And their unborn baby.

The darkening room now strangely quiet, Leopold finally mustered the courage to speak.

"Sir Richard, if I may," asked the Prince as respectfully as he could manage, "would it be possible for my wife to have some liquid nourishment, some broth, some sherry water, anything? She looks so pale and I would give anything to see some colour in her face."

Richard Croft turned brusquely toward the Prince, "My good sir, it is my opinion that the mother shall have nothing in her digestive tract during delivery that might affect the outcome of the pregnancy! The enlarged uterus can block the normal passage of nutrition," and his attentions returned to Princess Charlotte.

Leopold looked to his friend Baron Stockmar with a question on his face. Stockmar merely raised his eyebrows and shrugged his shoulders.

7 January 1814, Warwick House, London
Late evening

"Louise, I cannot believe they did not provide a proper birthday party!" Charlotte complained while her dresser attempted to remove the gala attire.

"My Princess, it is the dead of Winter and the snow is so tall."

"I feel like a shriveled lemon! If it had been His Pompous Highness's birthday, He would have commanded the sun to shine all night to melt the bloody snow! He has been in such a disagreeable and sulky state of late."

Louise smiled as she removed another piece of finery. She had taken care of Princess Charlotte since she was a child and knew that undressing her could be just as challenging as dressing her.

"I turned 18 today. A very special age. No party, no *cadeaux*–well, one precious *cadeau* from Lady Ashbrook–but nothing from Prinny save a trip to visit my mother. And she spent the entire day showing me the renovations on Connaught house. That was no party, I can tell you! At least I did not have to submit to Queen Granny's scrutiny. You know there are only two things I detest: one is apple tart, the other is Grandmama."

A pile of discarded clothing mounted.

"If I remember correctly, Princess, birthday 16 was *magnifique!*"

"Well, yes, *mais oui*, but that was two years ago!" and she dropped an undergarment on the floor. "None of my friends were in attendance this evening. If only Mercer could have been there, she always manages to keep me amused. I do believe more people attended my confirmation last month."

They both laughed.

"Not even Billy came, Louise."

The dresser stopped for a moment and looked up. "How are things going with you and your fiancé?"

Charlotte pulled her arm away, almost tearing a sleeve, "Ugh! How I detest this arranged marriage of diplomacy!" She flounced as she spoke, "He is uncouth, ungainly, ugly, and given to whiskey. I want to turn my face away from him when he speaks, but I resist all temptations to do so out of fear of retaliation by my fat, fat father. And, if that is not enough, Orange insists we spend the majority of the time in his precious little Holland, a very odd place, so boring and so different from London. I do believe it is the intention of the Prince Regent to remove me from this island by any possible means." She sniffled and turned away. "I have sought counsel from Earl Grey, and he acknowledges my right to refuse Prinny's commands where matters of the heart are concerned. Louise, I know it has been only a month, but I cannot imagine myself spending the rest of my life with Willy, let alone bearing him little princes and princesses!"

Her dresser chuckled at the suggestion. "But *chère* Charlotte, whomever you marry will become a king. You will have to submit to his will."

"A king?!" sputtered Charlotte. "Phooey! Never, never, never! He would be my subject but never my king!" She shrugged and crossed her arms, hugging herself tightly.

Louise tutted a few times, "My Princess, your deportment is not that of an heir to the throne. Your people will want a leader that is concerned and responsive to them. I have witnessed the consequences in my beloved France."

Charlotte relaxed her grip and faced the woman, "*Oui. Tu as raison, madame.* If only I could be more like Lizzy..."

"Who, my Princess?"

"Lizzy, Elizabeth Bennett," Louise shook her head minimally to express lack of understanding. "From *Pride and Prejudice,* Miss Austen's latest novel."

Mrs. Louis pursed her lips. "I was under the impression Her Highness fancied herself as Marianne Dashwood from *Sense and Sensibility.*"

"Yes, Louise, at one time I did find that we are quite alike in disposition; however, Marianne is an orphan–and I must confess there are times when I have wished to share that quality–but I still have both of my parents."

The dresser nodded her head with a bit of arched eyebrow and then continued to prepare her charge for sleep.

"Elizabeth allows herself to get trapped in an arranged marriage with a man she detests just so she can move out of her family's house. This Mr. Bingley has land and money, but he is rather plain and socially uncouth. Sound familiar?" She stopped to look at Louise, who was busy getting the Princess into her bedclothes. "But Lizzy meets Bingley's friend Darcy, who is handsome and dashing, but standoffish. Eventually, Elizabeth tells her father that she does not wish to marry Bingley and would instead prefer Darcy. Unfortunately, her mother strongly favours Mr. Bingley. Her father says that if she does not marry Mr. Bingley, her mother will never speak to her again, but if she does marry Bingley her father will never speak to her again because he wants to see her happy. If only I had a Darcy and my own father were as enlightened as Mr. Bennett." She giggled and Louise joined in.

By this time, the dresser had maneuvered Charlotte into the bed. As she placed the covers gently over the Princess, Louise cooed, "*Bon nuit, ma chère* Charlotte. Or should I start calling you Lizzy instead?" They both laughed.

"Tonight I shall dream of living at Longbourne and meeting my Mr. Darcy, Louise. *Bon nuit, mon amie!*"

"Tout les rêves douces, ma princesse."

Charlotte: The People's Princess

5 November 1817, Claremont House, Surrey
Early evening

Once again Leopold had been banished to the hallway. What little sunlight remained did not brighten the narrow room very much. At some point he would have to order the servants to light the lamps for the evening.

It had been two days since the beginning of Charlotte's labour pains and yet no baby had come forth. What kind of punishment is this for him and his bride? She was to be the woman who brought Britain back into the good graces of its people, rescuing it from the financial ruin wrought by her elders. Leopold planned to be the architect of this renaissance, and he could not stand to have his wife tortured so.

Count Stockmar bounded out of the room where Princess Charlotte lay. "Leo! Leo!" It was difficult to see in dusky hallway after leaving the somewhat brighter bedchamber.

Britain's Glory

"What news, Stocky?" Prince Leopold turned to face the Baron.

"Come quickly, Leo! The contractions are starting up again!"

The two men returned to Charlotte's chamber in hopes of seeing the delivery of the child at last.

Carlton House

12 June 1814, Carlton House, London
Evening

Prince George opened his extravagant London home to the European nobles living in London to celebrate of the end of the Napoleonic Wars. With the cessation of military operations on the Continent, Britain could concentrate more fully upon the ongoing skirmish with the United States.

As much as Charlotte detested her father, she did enjoy his lavish galas, and this promised to be the highlight of the season. She wore one of her most expensive gowns, pastel yellow with pearl beading and Brussels lace trim.

Princess Charlotte stood with Grand Duchess Catherine, sister of Russian Tsar Alexander. Catherine wore her traditional bonnet reminiscent of a coal bucket. Some suspected this design helped to hide or diminish her slightly Mongoloid features.

Charlotte: The People's Princess

"So tell me, my dear," the swarthy Russian Duchess purred, "how are things with you and your Orange?"

The Princess had been smiling at the crowd, but the question brought a frown to her face. "Honestly, Duchess, I don't know what to make of Billy. He is here, somewhere. The last time I saw him, he was drunk and disheveled."

"Tut, tut, my dear Princess. A man who is given to liquor so early in the evening does not deserve one such as yourself."

Charlotte turned to face Catherine. "Thank you, Duchess. His manners torment me and bring on plagues. I fear if this situation continues for very much longer, I shall have yet another violent orange attack."

The Duchess chuckled knowingly. "I am surprised that you are telling me your intimate feelings. You and I hardly know each other." She glanced sidelong around the edge of her bonnet to observe how Charlotte would react.

"Oh, Duchess," and she placed her hand on the woman's arm, "I feel like we have known each other forever and there is nothing I could keep from you." Charlotte looked into the black eyes of the Duchess, who smiled back with the grin of a cat holding a fresh mouse in its mouth. "It is evident that you have my best interests at heart, as I have yours," and she bent in to kiss her on the cold, dark cheek.

"Princess, you flatter me. I shall endeavor to travel to Holland to visit with you and your new family when such an excursion is possible."

Charlotte pulled her hand back, "I find his father an even bigger fool. Alas, I have no choice in this matter. My father, and only my father, may choose a husband for me."

"How dreary and backward. Your country is so modern in many ways, yet so provincial in many others."

The Princess nodded in agreement. "You cannot imagine the negotiations, treaties, contracts, counteroffers being submitted for approval. Only the King or Regent may permit my travel abroad or summon me back at a moment's notice. Only Parliament may permit me to leave the Country. Only the young frog prince can request... Not one version mentions my wishes or desires! It makes me feel much like the side of a beef at a butchery being haggled over!" and she threw her hands in the air as punctuation.

Catherine giggled quietly then continued, "I had a brief interaction with your rather disagreeable father the other day," and Charlotte giggled at this suggestion. "I asked him why he keeps you out of the public eye, and he told me you are too young to appear in society!" Charlotte snorted and Catherine looked at her. "I had the same reaction, but not so loud that he could hear me. Keeping you locked away is deplorable. You are so delightful and exuberant."

"Thank you, Duchess."

"So then I reminded him that you are not too young to be betrothed. He informed me you will not be married yet for a few years." The Princess glanced up at the ceiling. "To that I expressed my hope that when you are finally wedded you will be in charge of your person and no longer imprisoned."

"You are so correct! It does feel like imprisonment! Windsor is much like a nunnery."

The Duchess took a sip of her aperitif, "However, his belief is that when you are married, you will then be under your husband's command, just as you are under your father's now."

Charlotte made fists and thrust them downward. "Intolerable!"

"Precisely what your father said to the other guests regarding his interview with me!"

They both giggled.

"My dear Princess," the Duchess continued, eyeing Charlotte through narrow slits, "your father is most self-indulgent. His corpulence demonstrates an inability to control his primal urges. His attitude suggests a foolish belief that he is a demigod on Earth. His speech is crude, common and licentious. His eyes travel to places where a man's eyes should not go." Charlotte put her hand to her mouth. "However, his parties are *trop Beau Monde*! Let us see if we can find you a competitor for Holland. After all, it is such a small country. I'm sure you can do better than that!"

"Yes, oh, yes! The only way I could even tolerate such a land would be to make it more Londonish and... dandyish!" she giggled aloud under the observant eye of her Russian friend.

The two of them surveyed the young men in the room. The Duchess stood poised and aloof; Charlotte kept her hands clasped in the small of her back, pressing her pelvis forward awkwardly.

One of the passing partiers shouted to the Princess, "Don't desert your mother, dear!" to which she smiled and waved.

"Speaking of her, Your Highness, how is your mother?" the Duchess inquired.

The Princess threw her arms in the air with frustration.

"Charlotte, my dear, please keep your skirt down, one can see your drawers."

The Princess glanced down at her ankles. "Honestly, I care not if they can."

"Perhaps, Your Highness, your drawers are too long," and the Duchess pointed to the visible frills.

"I do not think so, and I have seen others wear theirs much longer!" Charlotte retorted. "Even so, they are bordered in Brussels lace!"

"I suppose if one is so disposed to display one's drawers in public, it does one right to make them handsome!" and the two giggled girlishly.

"Prinny and the old witch, the Merry Wife of Windsor—what I call Grandmama these days—have seen to it that I have no direct contact with my mother. I have no idea what they are so afraid of. The two of them have barred her from attending any state functions, including the Queen's drawing rooms. You know, there are two things I heartily detest: one is boiled mutton, the other is the Queen!"

"Charlotte!" remanded Catherine, "you are being rather disrespectful."

The Princess sighed, "That's what Papa says. 'Don't you know my mother is the Queen of England?'" she croaked in a deep, masculine-sounding voice. She then continued in her regular tone, "To which I reply, 'Don't you know my mother is the Princess of Wales? Or have you completely forgotten about her?'"

"Really, Your Highness! Are things that out of sorts?"

Charlotte raised her eyebrows, "My father has informants in his employ reporting back every little thing I might say or do. I would not be surprised if he knew exactly how long it takes to accomplish my toilet!"

They both laughed aloud.

"Be vigilant, my young friend. Many anxious hands will be thrust in your direction. Just make sure you know to whom the hand belongs before accepting its grasp."

Charlotte nodded as she attempted to decipher the advice. "Duchess, who is the young soldier speaking with the lady in blue way over there?"

Catherine turned to see whom Charlotte was indicating, "Oh, that is Prince Leopold George Christian Frederick of Saxe-Coburg-Saalfeld, my brother's Cavalry Officer."

"He's so tall and handsome. I wonder why the lady does not seem more interested in him."

"Because the real prize, my dear, is that one there," and she quickly pointed her silk-gloved finger. "Prince Friedrich Wilhelm Heinrich August von Preussen, nephew of *Friedrich der Große*."

"Yes, oh, yes," Charlotte cooed. "Can you arrange a meeting for me?"

"Certainly, my child," the Duchess smiled. "Anything to improve foreign relations."

Charlotte: The People's Princess

5 November 1817, Claremont House, Surrey
Early evening

As the light began to fade, the mood in Charlotte's chamber grew more tense. The attendant physicians stood about staring as if a great treasure was about to burst from her abdomen. Leo grasped his wife's clammy hand as a cold sweat broke out across her forehead.

"I'm sorry, Leo. I'm truly sorry." Her voice was barely audible.

He looked down at her humbled face. "About what, my sweet?"

"The baby!" She started heaving as if crying, but no tears appeared. "I fear we've lost the baby!" Her free hand balled into a fist.

The Prince continued to glance at his wife, "And what makes you say that, Charlotte?"

She pulled her hand back and touched her belly. "Until this morning I could feel the baby moving. Since about noontime I have felt nothing. No kicking, no shifting, nothing."

The physicians turned to look at one another with furrowed brows and widened eyes. Sir Richard maintained an upturned chin and placid expression.

Leo smiled at Charlotte. He took her hand and put it to his lips, "Now that we are certain we know how to do it, we shall soon give it another go."

She looked up and smiled with what little strength she had left. The fist relaxed and she allowed her body to go limp.

Britain's Glory

12 July 1814, Warwick House, London
Evening

Prince George followed the Great UP of Salisbury into the Princess's home. "Pray wait here, Bishop." The clergyman bowed ever-so-slightly and found the first chair to sit. George shuffled his bulk to where his daughter sat reading. "Please don't bother to get up for Us, Your Highness. We know you have not been in the best of health of late, or so the governess, Miss Knight, informs Us. It's your shin, or your ankle, or something..."

"It is my knee, Papa," and she began to stand. Her father stretched his arm out, open palm, commanding her to remain seated. "I was just about to..."

"We do not give a bleeding shit what you were about to," roared the Prince. "Once again, We must come to you, you sniveling twit of a twat, when it should be you who should attend the Prince Regent!" He snorted loudly and found a suitable chair. "Your presence was requested evening last, and all that showed up were your lame excuses! Well! If the mountain shall not come to Mohammed, as they say, Mohammed must climb the mountain."

"You've gotten it all muddled, Papa, it's..."

"Silence!" screamed George. "We shall speak and you shall listen! Got it?" Charlotte nodded her head gently. "You have recently written to Us demanding–DEMANDING–to examine the marriage contract between yourself and Orange. Your communication expressed the desire to know whether or not you shall receive a house upon marriage and if a provision could be inserted stipulating that you are not to leave Britain without your express consent. Is that your intention, dearest daughter?"

When Charlotte started to respond, her father shouted, "Do not speak! Merely nod your assent."

She nodded once. Multiple bleeding wounds and leech scars could be seen on his arms.

"Subsequent to that, you have written the Prince rejecting him and to provoke the dissolution of your engagement. Is that not so?" He stared at his daughter, awaiting a response. Again, she nodded once.

"Despite what you may think, there is no plan, nor conspiracy as you have suggested, to have you banished from your native land. However, it is a wife's duty to comply with her husband's wishes, and if the Prince of Orange decides to live in Holland, you shall follow him. Maybe his purse is large enough to build you the house you so desire. In the meantime, you are more than welcome to stay with Us at Carlton when you visit."

The Princess turned her head so that her father would not see the tears.

"The situation in this House is intolerable. You have no regard for the rules set forth by the Prince Regent regarding your behavior. And if that wasn't enough, your staff is aiding and abetting you in this little mutiny." He reached into a pocket and picked out an embroidered handkerchief. "Prussian princes and Russian army officers have no place in the home of the betrothed Princess Charlotte!" he dabbed at his moist forehead with the cloth. "Nor do you improve your public image by visiting these people at the Pulteney Hotel. We fear some of this has been the handiwork of that Russian witch duchess you are so keen on. We forbid you to have any further contact with any of the Russians!" The Princess exhaled audibly. "Sneaking men in and out at all hours gives you the appearance of the town whoreslut, not the royal heir. You shall marry William of Orange as We have commanded."

Charlotte put her hands over her ears as if that would negate the sentence.

"And as your staff has assisted in your treasonous affairs, I have summarily dismissed the lot and hired replacements." The Princess gasped in horror. "Despite the royal physicians' opinion that seaside air would be restorative, you shall proceed immediately to Cranbourne Lodge and spend the remainder of the Summer in isolation, save weekly visits from your grandmother. We pray you come to your senses regarding your marriage. That is all." He turned his head toward the front door and bellowed, "Bishop!"

When the Great UP entered the room, Charlotte glanced momentarily in his direction and then averted her gaze. The Prince Regent extended his blubbery arm and the Bishop assisted in raising the royal carcass. The two strode out without looking back.

Charlotte closed her eyes and clenched her fists. "God Almighty grant me patience!"

When she opened her eyes, she realised she was alone. Without saying another word, she quickly exited through the side door that opened onto Pall Mall.

After looking about for a few minutes, a man wearing a brown woolen suit strode up, "Miss, pardon, Miss, but I saw you from the window above. You seem to be in a bit of distress. Can I be of assistance?"

"Ummm, thank you Mr. ..."

"Collins, Miss." He was tall and slender, greying at the temples with careworn facial features. "Are you looking for someone?"

"Yes, um, no. I am looking to get to Oxford Street. Which way is it, if you please?"

"Not very familiar with London, are you? It can be a bit confusing, especially after dark. If I may suggest, Miss, a proper young lady such as yourself should not be walking on the street at this time of day. Shall I hail a cab for you?"

Charlotte: The People's Princess

Charlotte fiddled with her fingers, "Yes, if you believe that is best. Thank you."

Mr. Collins began to move off, "Follow me, Miss. I believe it will be easier to pick up a hackney-coach at Charing Cross."

She followed her guide through Cockspur Street and watched him flag down a passing carriage. He assisted Charlotte into the cab, her knee throbbed with heat and pain.

"Thank you, good sir," she bleated.

"No need to thank me, Miss. Just helping out a fellow good Christian in need," and he turned and walked back to Pall Mall, glancing over his shoulder to look at the vaguely-familiar stranger.

"Where to, chippie?" the Cockney driver asked. A rather dirty flat cap covered most of his forehead. Strawlike hair poked out in various directions.

"Oh, um," Charlotte had never taken a cab before, "to my mother's home, if you please."

The driver chuckled, "I'm afraid I hain't yet made yer mother's acquaintance, m'lady." His smile created many creases in his leathery face.

"No, I suppose not. If you take me to Oxford Street, it is near to Hyde Park. A handsome reward awaits if you can get me there with all speed possible."

"Ho! A 'andsome reward. Well, off we go, dearie. Hold tight!" and the driver lashed the horse.

As the carriage sped away, Charlotte looked out the rear and saw a young boy racing after them. He was probably eight or nine years old. She yanked the string to get the coachman's attention.

He turned round to face her, "Yes, dearie?"

"Driver," Charlotte yelled over the noise of the cobblestones, "I believe we are being pursued. Could you dispose of him, if you please?"

He halted the cab, and as he walked past the Princess, whip in hand, he stated, "I will protect you wiv the last drop o' me blood, I will." When the boy approached, the coachman raised the whip and began lashing at the child. "You go away, now, boy!" he screamed as he chased the lad.

The boy answered, "I only wanted to see her..."

"I don't give a shite what you was after! Go home, boy!" and he cracked the whip once more and the lad turned and ran off. The driver walked back to the cab and said, "Well now, seein' as that's all settled, we'll be now off to Oxford, m'lady."

"My gratitude to you, sir," Charlotte whispered.

When the carriage arrived at Connaught, the driver helped the Princess down. "Now, about the fare, young miss..."

"Oh, the Lady Fair? It's too early for that. Do you mean Bartholemew's?" Charlotte asked naively. "Not this evening, I am so sorry. Oh no, I couldn't possibly. I'm afraid I'm not in any proper state for a fair."

"No!" the coachman retorted with a hint of anger, "My fare, m'lady!" He held out his open hand. "Me bread. You promised a 'andsome reward fer fetchin' you here. Fair play's a jewel."

"Yes, of course. How silly of me. Please wait here. I do not have my purse with me."

"Oh, sure. I've got all hevenin'. Quoz," cracked the driver.

Charlotte limped up the stairs and knocked at the door. The page answered and bowed low. When the coachman saw this greeting, it dawned on him who the passenger had been.

"Mr. Stikeman, can you give me some coins to pay the hackney driver? He brought me here from Warwick."

The page reached into his purse pocket and withdrew three guineas. "Here, Your Highness, I believe this should cover it."

The Princess hobbled back down the stairs, "Thank you, Stikeman."

Charlotte: The People's Princess

When she presented the coins to the driver, he bowed low, "Yer 'ighness, pardon me for not recognisin' you straight off." He stood and took the guineas from her timidly.

"That's quite all right, sir."

"'iggins, Yer 'ighness," he bowed again, "'iggins, it is."

"Thank you, Mr. Higgins. But if I may ask you to wait, I have some correspondence to dash off that needs to be delivered immediately."

The driver bowed again, "Of course, Yer 'ighness. Anyfing. Anyfing at all."

Charlotte walked back to the house, her knee on fire. "Stikeman, is my mother at home?"

"No, Your Highness, she is on her way to dine in Blackheath this evening."

"Please order us up a meal, get me a pen and paper, then go retrieve her."

Mr. Stikeman bowed, "Yes, Your Highness. Immediately." He left Charlotte to gather her thoughts. When he returned, he handed her a slip of her mother's writing paper with a pen and ink. Then he rushed off to his horse.

Charlotte sat at the small desk in the entryway and scrawled:

> Connaught House, 12 July 1814, 7:00
>
> Duke of Sussex, Queen's House
>
> My dear uncle A_____,
>
> I have run off. Prinny is out of control. Please come to my mother's home as quickly as you can. I need your assistance greatly.
>
> Always your fondest niece,
>
> Charlotte P.

The Princess folded the paper and wrote her uncle's name. She walked outside and handed it to the coachman.

"Mr. Higgins, please take this note immediately to the Queen's House. It is for my uncle, the Duke of Sussex."

He bowed again. "Of course, Yer 'ighness. Straightaway, I will."

After he turned to go, Charlotte inquired, "Do I need to give you additional bread fare, sir?"

Higgins stopped and realised his luck this evening should not be pressed. Merely posting on his hackney-coach that he had transported the Princess Charlotte of Wales herself would allow him to see to a significant rise in his revenue. "Yer 'ighness has already compensated me, fank you, fankin' you very much!"

She waved at him from the top of the stairs as he sped off.

☙ 🕯 ❧

By 9:00, the Princess of Wales and the Duke of Sussex had arrived. Her friend Miss Mercer Elphinstone had heard what had happened and showed up earlier. A roast beef dinner had been laid out for them.

"Dearest uncle, please carve for us," Charlotte requested.

"My child, I am so weary, the only dish I am fit to carve is the soup!"

Everyone laughed.

As they ate, Charlotte narrated her tale with lively hand gestures:

"You cannot believe what that beast did! He showed up, unannounced, tipsy as usual. Without my consent, he fired all of my personal staff, accusing them of high treason! He forbade me to associate with Mercer. Imagine him deciding who my friends may be! He then dictated that I will be removed to Cranbourne Lodge, in the middle of nowhere Windsor Woods, where my only visitor is to be the Queen. It is bad enough he has made me his chess piece in European politics, fancying to move me off the board to Holland!" she pointed off somewhere toward the southwest. "They may attempt to wear me out by ill-treatment and represent I have changed my mind and consented. I could no longer stand these abuses and his tyranny, and I ran here to live with my mother, where I can feel safe and worthy, free to socialise with whomever I wish."

Princess Caroline of Wales stopped chewing and looked up, "My dear, I have not had the opportunity to inform you, but I am quitting England to travel abroad for a few years. I am so sorry."

"Well then, mother, I will have to negotiate directly with father." Charlotte turned to the Page. "Mr. Stikeman, would you be so good as to bring me some paper with a pen and ink again?"

The Page left and returned with the requested items.

Charlotte announced, "I shall explain that I wish to see my dear Mercer as often as I should like, and I wish to retain Mrs. Louis and Miss Knight in my employ." When she finished writing, she handed the missive to the Page. "Please take this to my father at Carlton. Thank you."

Mr. Stikeman took the letter and left. A minute later he returned, "Begging Your Highnesses' pardon, there is a line of coaches outside looking to speak with you."

"Are any of them the Royal Coach with my father?"

"No, Your Highness, I do not believe so."

Charlotte waved her hand, "Then please continue your assignment and instruct our visitors they may wait outside if they wish." The Page turned and left again.

Her mother admonished, "Charlotte! It is not polite to leave a gentleman caller out in the weather."

"Mother, I do not wish to see anyone else this evening, save father."

"You know, Charlotte," her uncle spoke, "if the Prince Regent authorises a warrant for your detention, you would have no recourse. By law, the Monarch, or Regent in this case, has absolute power to dispose of persons under age who are part of the Royal Family." The Princess tilted her head and jutted her chin slightly. "I would advise you to return to Warwick with as much speed and as little noise as possible."

Miss Elphinstone nodded in agreement and Princess Caroline joined in, "I believe your uncle is quite correct, my daughter. It might be better than the public observing you being hauled away kicking and screaming."

Charlotte turned her neck this way and that. "In case you have all lost your sense of time, my 18th birthday occurred this past January, and I am no longer 'under age,' as you say. Despite my mad conduct, I do believe I am not quite ready neither to submit nor surrender. I shall wait for father's reply."

ଓ ঃ ୨୦

When Prince George left Warwick House, he returned to Carlton for an evening of cards with his oldest brother, the Duke of York. He received Charlotte's letter, laughed aloud and continued to play. After a while, he scribbled a few things on the paper and handed it to his brother.

"Here, take this to the witch's house and let the little bitch see how the game is played!"

The Duke did as he was asked. However, he was not given entrance at Connaught and could only hand the letter to the Page.

The Princess glanced at her father's scrawlings and let out a cry of exasperation. "He says he will agree to Mercer and nothing more! What a pompous, obstinate bastard!"

"Charlotte, your father may be many things," Caroline said with a bit of sarcasm, "and most are not repeatable in proper company. However, he is sitting as Prince Regent and must be respected as such."

"I will give him that respect when he earns it from me!"

"Daughter, I believe the hour is late, you are tired and distressed. Your eyes are red and bleary. Please return to Warwick before it is too late and we cannot repair the damage."

"Mother, I have no intention of giving in. Forgive me if I am intruding in your home, but I shall not return to mine until father desists from his silly ranting."

"Charlotte, if I might," it was the voice of Mercer Elphinstone but unusually meek. "It is almost dawn and in a few hours the empty street and park will be full of people. There is to be a by-election today, and folks will be walking directly past that window to vote. If you should open the window, make your grievances known and proclaim your predicament directly to the people of London, they will all rise in your behalf."

The Princess smiled and a light sparkled in her eyes. "And why should they not?" she mused.

"Dearest Charlotte," her uncle beseeched, "should you follow the course described by Miss Elphinstone, the mob would most likely march on Carlton demanding your father's head. If they are not mollified directly, they might even tear the building down in anger. The dragoons would have to be called in to quell the unrest, blood will be shed, and even if you lived a full century hence, it shall not be forgotten that your choice to run off was the cause of the disturbance, you may depend on it. Such is our people's horror of bloodshed, you would never get over it." He rested his hands in his lap genteelly.

She mulled this over and replied, "Oh uncle, you are always so wise! That is why I knew to summon you in my hour of need." He smiled. "I suppose I should present myself to the Prince Regent, but this shall be done on my terms." She clucked her tongue. "I am a princess, second in line to the throne of Britain and should be treated as such. Mr. Stikeman, please convey a message to His Royal Highness that I shall appear at Carlton if he sends the Royal Coach."

The Page bowed and ran off. Everyone else raised their eyebrows in surprise.

Charlotte handed the paper, pen and ink to her uncle. "My dear, would you be so kind to compose for me? I am too distraught."

"Of course, my child. What is your wish?"

She touched a finger to her lips in thought. "Please write something to the effect that I have no intention nor inclination to marry the spider-legged Prince of Orange, and should there be any announcement of such a match, it must be understood that it is without my consent and wholly against my will. Yes, I believe that is all. Please have the staff make copies for all here. I shall sign them all so that my thoughts are well known."

The Duke of Sussex had a small tear in his eye. "I had no idea you had so much good in you, my dear."

Shortly, the Royal Coach arrived. The Duke of York appeared and extended his hand to Charlotte. She accepted her uncle's hand and climbed into the carriage. The Duke of Sussex followed her in.

The coach drove down Park Lane across to Pall Mall and into Carlton. Passers-by strained to get a look at the passengers. Once the carriage arrived, the Duke of York hopped out to announce the arrival of the Princess. Nearly an hour later, he returned to admit his niece to the house.

5 November 1817, Claremont House, Surrey
Evening

"I am so sorry to be eating in front of you, my sweet," Prince Leo picked at his supper while his wife looked on. Light from the lamp flickered about, casting moving shadows.

"That's fine, Leo, you need your nourishment."

"But Charlotte, you haven't had anything for two days. Stockmar is not sure what Sir Richard has in mind for you, but this all seems very wrong to me." He clenched his cheek muscles to display concern and then picked up a piece of soggy bread.

"The accoucheur is in charge now, my dear." She tried to smile with what little strength she had. "Besides, I'm feeling ill more than anything and not very hungry any— Mmmmp!"

Britain's Glory

Leopold stood up quickly, knocking a dish to the floor. "What is happening?"

Charlotte screamed in pain and placed a hand on her belly. "The contractions have returned."

"Croft!" the Prince bellowed.

31 July 1814, Cranbourne Lodge, Windsor Great Park
Mid-afternoon

For a Royal country home, Cranbourne Lodge did not receive the same attention and appointments as the castle up the hill. Charlotte sat in the relatively spartan ground floor drawing room writing her correspondence.

"We see country life has not killed you as of yet," Prince George sneered as he entered, unbuttoned the grey tweed riding coat and lowered himself onto a chaise with the assistance of the Great UP. The bishop then stood off to the side farthest from the Princess.

"Papa, what a surprise," Charlotte stated flatly and stood with both hands clasped behind her.

George cleared his throat and proceeded, "We have come to tell you that in a week's time, your bloated mother will be

Charlotte: The People's Princess

leaving for the Continent, and We believe you might like to see her before she leaves."

"Yes, that would be desirable." Still with no emotion. "Will she be coming here?"

Her father nearly choked, "No, no, no, no, no! You shall go to London. Heavens, We would not want her here!"

"Oh, Papa! A trip to London?" now she was excited. "I did believe you were going to keep me in this prison until my coronation."

The Prince grimaced at the suggestion. "Don't get your hopes up too high. You will be chaperoned," and he indicated the Bishop, "so that you will not have any undesirable interactions with others." The Bishop nodded in agreement. "It has come to Our attention that you have surreptitiously entertained the Princes Augustus of Prussia and Leopold of Coburg. Augustus is twice your age, already married and a bloody fool. Coburg, who, incidentally, at least has the courage the write to Us directly to ask for your hand, is churchmouse poor and a bloody fool. It can be surmised that you were introduced to Augustus by the Russian Duchess. How did you find the young Coburg?"

Charlotte fluttered her eyes. "He... opened a door for me once and has been smitten ever since."

What the Princess did not offer was that the door was at the Pulteney Hotel, where she had gone to spend time with Prince Augustus and Duchess Caroline. When they learned that Prince William of Orange was also in the building, Charlotte and her attendant slipped out a side door. Leopold just happened to be standing by it in his formal cavalry uniform. He asked if he could be of assistance and Charlotte introduced herself and asked if he could see them to their carriage. The Prince obliged. Charlotte thanked him and asked his name. When she found out he was a prince, she then admonished him for not calling upon her as all the other Princes had. He apologised and asked if he could have a chance to correct his error. She agreed nonchalantly as her carriage moved off.

"But I do not care for him, he does not suit my taste," she bluffed.

"You, however, appear to suit his."

"Oh?"

"Yes," the Prince puffed. "The young prince has written to Us in such broken language such that I cannot decipher whether he is attempting to court the Prince Regent or his daughter." Charlotte giggled but then quickly regained her composure. "For the time, We will proceed under the assumption that he desires an arrangement with you. He, at least, appears to be a gentlemanly young man, in contrast with the Prussian, who is neither gentlemanly nor young."

She squinted at him.

"You might also be happy to know that your Uncle Augustus has taken up your cause in Parliament." Charlotte now paid attention. "He introduced a handful of questions regarding your further care and handling. Unfortunately for you, political opposition caused him to withdraw, and not even your precious Earl Grey could stand up for you. How sad."

Her shoulders slumped upon hearing this.

"Prepare to leave in the morning for London. And don't get any silly ideas. Your party shall have a dozen eyes upon you, and you shan't be left alone for a moment. Upon your return, We shall discuss plans to go to the seaside. Apparently the physicians believe your health is suffering here and a holiday by the sea is one thing your uncle managed to get approved."

"Brighton? I get to see Brighton?" her childlike curiosity eclipsed her staid manner. The Prince had lavishly renovated the old oceanfront pavilion with Asian motifs and it was widely known to be stunning.

"Ha, ha, ha, ha–no. Brighton is *Our* town. We would not let you within 20 miles of it. Your grandmother is willing to let you use Gloucester Lodge in Weymouth."

Charlotte stamped. "That's not fair! It's odious and all the way out in bloody Dorset!"

Charlotte: The People's Princess

The Prince shook a finger at her, "Tut, tut, young lady. Watch your bloody language." He then reached inside the coat for one of his silk handkerchiefs.

She shook her fists. "May I at least bring Mercer along for companionship?"

George dabbed his moist forehead as he spoke. "I'm afraid not. Lord Keith told me he did not want his eligible young daughter to spend so much time in isolation with you. He is worried she might never find a suitable husband if she is away for such a length of time."

She screamed in frustration. "By the time I get out there, the summer will be over and I will have no one to spend the time with."

"Not to worry, my child. You shall never–NEVER–be alone for a moment." With a flurry of his handkerchief, the Bishop assisted the Prince to rise, and they both waddled out, leaving Charlotte to complete her correspondence with a smirk on her face.

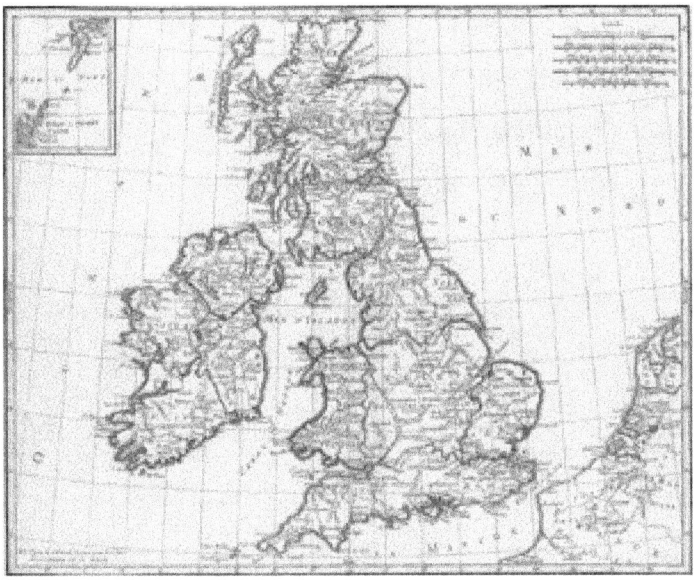

Britain's Glory

5 November 1817, Claremont House, Surrey
Evening

Prince Leo stood by his wife, holding her hand as she squeezed and squeezed again and again. Sweat dribbled off her and further dampened the sheets.

"Aaaaarrhhh!" she screamed, "It hurts, Leo! It hurts!"

"Where is the Brunswick heart that pledged neither to bawl or shriek?" he purred.

"In bloody Brunswick!" she screamed.

"Try to think of how your own mother went through this very same thing to bring you into the world." Leopold focused on her every breath.

"I am thinking she should have bloody given up… Aaaaaahhh!… never given birth… Uhhhhh!… That is what I am thinking, bloody hell!"

"Charlotte," and he squeezed her hand in an attempt to comfort her, "had you never been born I would not have the joy of sharing this with you now."

"Stop the pain, Leo! Stop the pain!"

He smiled, "The pain will soon be gone, my love."

"Not soon enough! Aaaaaaarrrhhh!"

11 November 1814, aboard the *Royal Charlotte*, off Weymouth
Afternoon

The ship-rigged, three-masted vessel had originally been designed for Princess Charlotte's great-grandmother, Queen Caroline, and named in her honour. Later it served to transport her grandmother, Queen Charlotte, from her home in Germany to England for the marriage to her grandfather, George III. At that time it was re-christened for her.

Charlotte and Margaret sat amid deck sharing a picnic lunch while Captain George Scott observed them from the bridge above. Dressed more for a day on the grass, in their long, Tudor-style frocks, they looked out over the calm waters of the Channel as the breeze played with their hair and bonnets. Near the rail sat Bishop Fisher, who had escorted Miss Elphinstone to Weymouth. Dressed in his black robes, hands folded across his great belly, he sniffed at the salty air with his eyes closed and a hint of a smile.

"How delightfully refreshing to see you again, Margaret Mercer! It was so kind of our fathers to allow this happy reunion," Charlotte giggled to her friend as the yacht rocked gently.

"Yes, I have missed you most excruciatingly! London is so boring without your glowing presence, my dear C."

A servant removed the luncheon plates and refilled their glasses with rose water.

"Thank you, my dear M. I imagine the earth still turns and the sun still rises and sets," the Princess said with a hint of mischief.

"But not as beautifully, Your Highness," and Mercer lifted her glass in a mock toast.

"Well, if my behavior suits big Prinny, I shall be at Windsor for Christmas, and we can visit there as well." The two girls laughed and touched hands. "So, M, how is husband hunting going? Are we betrothed yet?"

Mercer scrunched her face in mock desperation, "There are no good men left, C. They're all pursuing you!" and she pointed a wiggling finger at her friend.

"Someday soon I shall choose the lucky bastard who may wed me and then you can have your pick of the left-overs!" Again they laughed.

"Please tell me what has been happening," Mercer begged. "I am dieing of curiosity!"

"As long as the Great UP is out of earshot." They turned to look at the Bishop, who appeared asleep. They looked at each other and nodded. "The Great UP is out!"

Mercer touched Charlotte's wrist, "Pray begin."

"Oh, where to begin, there is so much to tell." She looked up to the cloud-filled heavens for inspiration then back to her friend. "To start with, they assigned me a coven of nasty, ugly, old women as traveling companions, and on the ride down, every time we stopped to change horses or get water, people would gather round. I don't know how the news spread so quickly, but they kept coming up to our party smiling, cheering and doffing their hats."

"You're such a popular princess, C!"

"I suppose, but it got a bit thick when we reached Salisbury and I tried to get to the inn. A crowd had formed around the carriage, and I had to press through the bodies to get inside. Even in my room they would not leave me alone, standing outside chanting my name. I stood at the window with a light for the longest time so they could see me."

"The price of fame, I guess."

"And the next day we rode on to Puddletown, and the roads were choked with even more people. Wherever do they come from? That ghastly General Garth, you know the general?" Mercer nodded, "had hired a house for us. Unfortunately, bony old Lady Rosslyn was there with her bratty nieces–Famine and the Consequences, I call them–but they left before dinner. Thank goodness! The most peculiar young boy captured my heart. He was the most loveliest thing!" She smiled slightly at the thought. "At first the General introduced him as an adopted nephew, but later he revealed that the boy was his own from my dear Aunt Sophia! It was so embarrassing! Perhaps he was trying to get back at my aunt by torturing me with this sad news. And the poor boy! Everyone in Weymouth knows about it too."

"I'm sure he'll outgrow it. Boys seem to have less of a care for idle chatter."

"So true. When we finally reached the lodge, some military band prattled on and on while another throng of masses attempted to get just a glimpse of me!"

Her friend tutted, "Popular Princess, Popular Princess."

Charlotte slapped at Mercer, "It's not funny!"

"It must be so difficult being you, Charlotte, Your Highness, I mean Your Princess-ship."

"Knock off, Mercer!"

"And speaking of Princess ships, I noticed even this yacht is named for you!"

"It is not!" she sputtered, "It is my granny's vessel; it's her name, not mine."

"Still your name, dear heart," and she grabbed Charlotte's fluttering hand. "Oh, my! What happened to the stone?" Mercer stared at the ring given to the Princess by her Prussian suitor, Augustus. A heart-shaped cavity had previously held a turquoise.

"I wish I knew! I didn't notice for a long time. Looked everywhere. For such an apparent trifle, it had quite an effect on me. I have cried bitterly over this and I fear it is an omen. A bad, bad omen. What do you think, M?"

"A woman quite frequently loses her heart *to* a man," she mused, "which is bad enough, but this is the first I have heard of a woman losing her heart *from* a man."

Charlotte stuck her tongue out at her playfully.

"What have you heard from the Prince?" Mercer inquired.

"Nothing, Miss E., nothing since he left England. I can't even read the old letters because I burned them for fear of Prinny finding them. I have imagined Augustus sailing back on his royal vessel, landing at Brighton, pressing to ask the Prince Regent for my hand. But stupid Prinny would most likely refuse out of spite. We would have to appeal directly to Parliament, which would make the newspapers. The people would support me and Papa would have to give in. Don't you think so, M?"

"Well, my dearest C," Mercer hesitated, "the chatter around town is that Prince Augustus has married some Miss Rumbold or other and got himself appointed Governor of Saxony. I don't think he's coming back for you any time soon, sweet. Sorry."

Charlotte stiffened her lip. "*Voilà tout.* I suppose I might just marry anyone to get away from Prinny's tyranny. Either that or I will have to dispatch myself like Queen Dido, now that I have lost my Æneas. Do you know of any available princes?"

Mercer laughed, "Me? Know princes? My dear, that is your department. I'm not allowed to forage above the level of Knight. The daughter of a lowly admiral cannot cast her eyes up to the royals," she scoffed. "What about the other one? Coburg? What have you heard from him?"

The Princess cast her eyes down, "Not as much as Papa has. Leopold seems to think the way to me is through my father's vanity. Perhaps he is correct. He would at least be preferable to any of the other princes I've encountered." She quickly looked up at her friend. "Mercer! I read recently of two princes quarreling at the Vienna Congress. Do you think it could have been Augustus and Leopold fighting over me?"

"That must be it, Your Highness," Mercer mocked. "If you could see the way the two of them bristled with jealousy whenever they have met."

"Please be gentle with me, Mercer. This seaside venture is to restore my ailing health, not to destroy what's left of my pride."

"I am so sorry, C. I didn't mean anything."

"Apology accepted." She took a sip of the rose water. "Oh! M, I almost forgot to tell you. Earlier month we went to visit one of those old castles around here—I can't remember which one—but the day was nearly ruined by a horrible storm. At one point I said, 'It rains like the very devil!' and one of the ladies in the crowd shouted, 'I trust Your Highness will never reign so.' Rain–reign. Get it?"

"Oh, I got it, C. I got it. By the way, how is the social life out here in the provinces?"

Charlotte's face lit up. "It's not exactly London, but it is so far superior to Cranbourne! There's a theatre, they have dances, and I even get to host a few dinners. Unfortunately, the clergy here leave me pining for Westminster."

"How so?"

"Well, first off, the Great UP has been on holiday here with his family, and one Sunday they let him deliver the homily. My dearest, M! I had never heard the man preach before. All

I've ever heard him do is ramble on about my schoolwork. He has the mousiest voice and such horrid delivery he could ruin the best sermon ever written!"

"Squeak, squeak, squawk!" Mercer made noises.

"Oh, a squawk every so often might have broken up the monotony," and she rolled her eyes upward. "But as horrible as the BishUP was, nothing could touch the antics of the famous Dr. Dupré."

"*The* Dr. Dupré?" she mocked.

"The very one," Charlotte continued, "Most likely famous in his own mind only. You can't believe how he filled up almost an entire hour with circular repetitions and obvious blunders! He had Noah in the Garden of Eden, and Job in the whale." Mercer laughed cautiously and Charlotte gazed upward in mock solemnity. "I know! How silly! But the worst part was that at one point he kept repeating the same treacle over and over and over, as if he was waiting for some divine spark."

"Sounds simply dreadful. Perhaps a lightning spark would have been preferable." She touched a finger to her temple and stuck out her tongue.

"Thank heaven I had the sense to wear one of those huge poke-bonnets the Duchess Caroline gave me and I could turn my head inside of it so that no one could see me giggling."

"I'm sure you weren't the only one suppressing laughter, C."

"I suppose not, but I would have died of embarrassment to look round. *Espérance et constance*, I say." She lifted her chin with purpose.

"An excellent credo, *ma chère*."

"With nothing but crocodile luck out here, I need all the encouragement I can muster. Things would have probably been much better at Brighton."

"And why are we not at Brighton?"

"Only the heavens and Prinny know. I fear that it is my own want of going to Brighton that keeps him from allowing it. Miserable sod."

"Oh, dear," Mercer smirked at Charlotte's impudence.

"Word around is that the bastard is still trying to divorce Mama so that he can produce a rightful male heir to supersede me." She fiddled with her fingers aggressively. "It would be my undoing if he is successful."

"Yes," Mercer agreed nonchalantly and then changed the subject quickly. "Have you had any notable callers?"

"Aside from family and staff, not so much. Oh! One day I was walking along the beach and some children climbed the hill above to try to get a look at me. With every step they loosened pebbles that tumbled down, raining on me. While it is flattering–and charming in a way–I did not wish to die in an avalanche of stones, so I called up to them, 'Princess Charlotte is made of ginger-bread, you know. If you continue pelting her with pebbles, you shall break her.'"

Mercer put her hand to her mouth in awe. "You didn't!"

"I did!" Charlotte shot back. "And a good thing too. They all shrieked and ran off."

"Sounds like jolly fun."

"It was, dearest M, it was."

The two friends stared at each other for a while, smiling. Suddenly, Charlotte looked away.

"M! Look!" The Princess pointed at a long boat that had pulled up beside the yacht. "Did your father order this?"

Mercer laughed. "I don't think so, C."

"Ahoy Princess!" shouted the captain from the long boat. "I am Captain Nixon. The *HMS Leviathan* wishes to pay respect to Your Highness." He pointed at a naval vessel sitting a ways off.

Charlotte shaded her eyes with one and to get a better look at the *Leviathan*, then glanced at Mercer with a surprised look and finally turned to Captain Nixon. "I thank you, good captain. Yours seems a very fine ship of war. I should very much like to go aboard her. Will you do us the honour of allowing us to inspect your fine vessel?"

"How many of you are there?"

"Myself, the daughter of Admiral Elphinstone and the Bishop of Salisbury, our chaperone."

"I believe we can accommodate you, Your Highness. Please board when ready."

"Young lady," the old bishop croaked, "do you not think your father would disapprove of you sailing in a small, open boat like that?"

Charlotte bristled, "Queen Elizabeth took great delight in her navy and was not afraid to go on board a man of war in an open boat. I shall follow her example without fear." She turned to the long boat and shouted, "Captain Nixon, I am not only desirous but determined to inspect your vessel."

"Captain Scott," Nixon shouted, "may I have your leave to transport the Princess and her companions to my ship of war for proper inspection?"

Scott glanced down and waved his hand twice in acknowledgment.

The three of them climbed down the rope ladder to the long boat. The out-of-breath bishop shook hands with the ship captain. Nixon clasped Mercer's hand gently and kissed it lightly. "Miss Elphinstone, it is an honour to meet you. While I have not served with your esteemed father, I have followed his career and studied his strategies."

Mercer turned to Charlotte and flashed a mischievous grin. "Why Captain Nixon, how kind of you to say so. At home we grow weary hearing of his naval exploits over dinner. By the way, Captain Nixon, are you a married man?" and she flashed her eyelashes at him.

The captain blushed and averted his gaze, "Yes, Miss, I am."

Mercer looked backed at her friend raised her eyebrows and shrugged as if to say, "Well, at least I tried."

The Channel water splashed over the sides, causing their clothes to get somewhat soaked. Once alongside the *Leviathan*, the crew lowered a chair to bring up the young women.

"Princess, if you will," the captain indicated the chair.

Charlotte smiled cryptically. "Captain Nixon, I thank you, but I wish to ascend proper as would a sailor." She stood up, the captain extended his hand, and Charlotte stepped over to the ledge. "Pray follow me and take care of my clothes." The two grabbed the wood and rope ladder, the captain following Charlotte, and climbed up the side of the ship while Mercer and the bishop were brought aboard by chair.

"I see your knee has improved, Your Highness," Mercer teased.

The captain introduced his officers. Charlotte looked fore and aft.

"How large and sturdy your vessel is! We might as well call it the 'Wooden Walls of Old England.'" A few people laughed. "How many guns onboard your ship, Captain?"

"We sail with a complement of 74 cannons, Your Highness."

"74... Let's see... That makes this a third-class ship, if I remember correctly."

"Correct, Your highness. We are ranked third-class by our guns, but first-rate by our crew."

The crew cheered the compliment.

"Well, then, Captain, I shall not be satisfied until I have seen every accessible part of this first-rate ship."

Over the next hour, the captain showed the visitors around the berths, powder magazines, cargo hold, and cabins. Princess Charlotte played her part and demonstrated her additional knowledge of sailing vessels. Captain Nixon smiled with pride.

Britain's Glory

Standing on the main deck, ready to depart, the Princess turned to the captain. "Captain Nixon, we thank you heartily for the gracious tour of your vessel. It is refreshing to see the safety of our nation in such good hands. I wish to present your crew with a purse to divide amongst them as a small demonstration of gratitude." She handed the captain a sack of coins.

The crew presented a royal salute and cheered the party, who then departed for the long boat and returned to the royal yacht.

5 November 1817, Claremont House, Surrey
Evening

"Your Highness, things will proceed apace if you can assist us and push the baby out," Sir Richard Croft instructed.

Charlotte looked up at her husband with fear and Leopold turned to the accoucheur, "Sir Richard, she has no resources left. No strength." Croft continued to stare at Charlotte's groin. "Without nourishment, Charlotte is unable to... She hasn't eaten in two days!"

"And with good reason, Your Highness." He looked up to speak to the Prince. "If the uterus becomes overly engorged, it might harm the Princess."

Leopold clenched and unclenched his fists while inhaling and exhaling.

Sir Richard turned back to Charlotte, "Princess, if you are unable to push, there is very little I can do at this time. We will have to wait."

25 December 1814, Windsor Castle
Afternoon

The Prince Regent arrived at Windsor with all the pomp and fanfare he so loved. Decorated and festooned for the Holiday, the castle exuded a warmth not usually found within its chilly, granite walls. Wearing the military traveling clothes he enjoyed, George marched into the cavernous family room, where most of the Royal Family sat talking. After looking about and greeting his family, he looked at his daughter and commanded, "Princess Charlotte, Princess Mary, please accompany Us."

Long shadows of the winter afternoon fell across the silenced room. Both niece and aunt wore winter woolens because of the cold air of the old castle. Charlotte and Mary exchanged blank looks, stood and followed Prince George. He waddled to Mary's private chamber, less plush than most because she was the youngest of the royal siblings, ushered the two women inside and closed the door.

"Charlotte," he began as he lowered his girth into a comfy chair, "We want to reassure you that while We are still alive, you have nothing to worry about with regard to the royal succession." The Prince turned to look out the window, squinting in the waning light of the day. "However, your mother has recently been reasserting the validity of that young urchin she cherishes, claiming he would be the rightful heir to succeed Us."

"That is not totally surprising, father. Mother has frequently announced her preference for little Willikin over me. She has said it time and time again, even directly in front of me."

"That does not surprise Us," George snorted.

"Until he was five years old, he slept in the same bed with her, and now she has him sleeping in a smaller bed next to hers."

The Prince shuddered. "We have only slept in the same bed with Caroline for two nights and it was pure torture, We tell you plainly. The stench alone is enough to make a proud Englishman suffer. That young man is quite brave to have survived this long under those conditions."

Mary spoke, "At least it keeps other men out of her chamber at night!"

Both George and Charlotte turned sharply to look at Mary. She glanced downward.

"Speaking of other men in the bedchamber," Prince George now turned to Charlotte, "are you familiar with a certain officer in the 18th Hussars, stationed here at Windsor?"

"Yes, father," Charlotte admitted, "and I am not ashamed of my relationship with Mr. Hesse." She looked at her father, expecting retribution, but when none came she continued, "As a lieutenant of the guard, he has ridden beside my carriage and we have exchanged words. We have even exchanged letters and small gifts, as friends often do."

"And...?" George goaded, "bedchamber?"

Charlotte cocked her head as she considered what her father was suggesting. Finally it hit her. "Oh, that. Once, while visiting mother at Kensington, she locked Mr. Hesse and myself in her bedchamber and screamed through the door to us, '*A present je vous laisse, amusez-vous bien.*'"

Her aunt Mary looked somewhat shocked.

"Who knows what would have become of me if he had not behaved with such respect. He was gentleman and officer both," Charlotte explained.

George cleared his throat, "Dear child, it is Providence alone that has saved you." He glanced haughtily at his daughter. "Lieutenant Hesse is well-known around here for his lack of restraint with young ladies. Things could have gone much worse for you. A most infamous and villainous affair. Are you still fond of him?"

"As a friend," she blurted, "And only as a friend, Papa."

"We want to believe you, Charlotte, but it is society at large that is the concern. Is your Uncle Frederick aware of this?"

"I do not believe so, father. Why?"

"It would seem obvious that his interests lay with his sister–your misbegotten mother–and he would do whatever it takes to discredit you and make little What's-his-name's claim stronger, including falsifying information about the bastard's parentage." He stared directly at his daughter. "Your mother alerted Us to the fact that Frederick has been telling people that the boy is hers."

"Yes, I have heard that as well. But what can we do? Even if the child is hers, it is certainly not yours."

"Ugghh," the Prince exhaled in exasperation, "It is to be hoped not, but there are many other possible candidates, and it would seem that no one would know the roster better than you."

"George!" Princess Mary exclaimed, "she was but a child."

"But a bright and observant child. Let us see. It is amazing that someone so repulsive and vile can still manage to attract so many men willingly. How many of your mother's dalliances can you recall?"

"I object to this line of questioning," Mary interrupted. "You are commanding your daughter to bear witness against her own mother!"

"Yes, We do believe you are correct, dear sister, but it is of little importance because the question comes directly from the Prince Regent, not her father. Pray answer, child."

Charlotte looked at her aunt and then up at the ceiling for inspiration, "The very first I can recall was a portrait painter. I can't recall his name. She would spend hours with him, sitting for that horrid painting, and then he would ask to remain for the night instead of having to drive home in the dark."

"Interesting. Sir Thomas Lawrence, if memory serves. And you are quite correct. The portrait is hideous, as would be any likeness of that woman."

"Yes, that's it. Sir Thomas. And she was quite fond of naval officers. There was a secretary fellow..."

"George Canning."

"I suppose. And two handsome captains: Smith and Manby. Mama even said you visited her once or twice during that time, and she tells some people that you are the boy's father."

"Impossible! Impossible!" He swatted his knee with a hand in frustration. "There has been no contact with her since just after our marriage. You know, she will say anything to anyone who will listen. But who was the one who could have been the Whatsit child's father?"

"Oh, Papa, that was ever so long ago. I was so young. How can you expect me to..."

"Charlotte!" bellowed her father.

"Manby, Your Highness. It would have been Captain Manby of the *HMS Africaine*."

"Thank you." The Prince turned his head away. "Now, the object of this interview is not to reprimand you for your unseemly conduct, but rather to strategise a plan of action to clean up this sordid mess before your good name is besmirched. Things would have been far simpler if only you had chosen to be born male instead of a member of the weaker sex. Whatever possessed you to make such an improper choice?"

Charlotte giggled, "I do believe the gender of the child is determined by the parents, not the baby itself, Your Highness. At least that's what my educators taught me."

"Idiots and fools all!" George slapped at his head in a mocking manner. He then turned to glare directly at Charlotte, "It is difficult to believe that you could not see what your mother intended by locking you and Mr. Hesse in her bedchamber." He turned away again. "However, you are still young and immature."

Charlotte started to speak then thought better of it.

"It would seem that she was attempting to discredit you so that her own issue, Mordred..."

"William, Papa."

"Yes, well, whomever... That Boy will trump your place in line for the throne. We need to assure your chastity and not allow that witch to work her blackest magic. We are advising you to recover, by any means necessary, all letters, communications and gifts from Mr. Hesse so that he cannot hold them as blackmail." His squinted gaze focused sharply on Charlotte. "Is that understood?"

"Yes, Papa. I shall have Mercer intercede for me so that there is no further suggestion of wrong-doing."

"Wise plan, child. It is becoming apparent that you might yet be fit for this job... someday." He smiled.

"Not for a very long time, Papa."

"Good! We like the sound of that! Now, We must return to London." He stood.

"But Papa, it is Christmas!"

The Prince had started walking toward the door. He stopped and turned, "Oh, yes. Happy Christmas to you both," and he continued out of the chamber.

"Happy Christmas, Papa," Charlotte whispered. She then looked her aunt. "Aunt Mary, I cannot believe such innocent behavior can lead to evil thoughts."

"My beautiful niece, you have so much to learn about being born into this bedeviled family. People loathe us for whom we are, envy us for what we have, detest us for what we do, and yet they still want to be one of us. Any opportunity to bring us a rung lower brings them one rung closer. We have an added burden of appearing correct in public at all times so that this type of innuendo can be avoided, especially those who are in direct line for the throne." She studied Charlotte's features, noticing how similar they were to her own. "Your grandfather expects the highest morals from his daughters, yet the sons conduct themselves like jungle beasts on the plains of Africa." She halted, inhaled and exhaled. "I apologise, sweet Charlotte, for ranting so. Your home life was ever so different from mine. We shall see this through together."

"I never intended to hurt anyone, Aunt Mary. I feel as though I have let Papa down, myself down, and possibly the worst, let our country down." She began to tear.

Her aunt hugged her lightly, "Child, if this is the worst of your offences, the country will be much better off when you ascend the throne." She kissed her niece gently on the forehead brushing aside the brunette ringlets. "And the sooner, the better. What does your mother think of your Orange? Does she want you to follow through on the arranged marriage?"

"As you probably know, my mother is one of the most difficult people to understand. Her words frequently do not follow her actions. I remember the way she used to treat poor Lady Douglas. In private, mother showered the woman with praises galore, but as soon as another person was in their presence, her whole attitude shifted, and Lady Douglas became the object of mother's vicious hen pecking."

"She is a trifle hard to figure."

"As far as the Little Frog, mother was against William at the start because her House of Brunswick opposed the House of Orange vehemently. However, over time I believe she made every possible attempt to hate him less so that by the time I put an end to the foolishness, she had quite adjusted to the inevitability."

"Far better than you, I'm afraid." They laughed together.

Charlotte stopped abruptly, "Aunt Mary, do you suppose Prinny is considering reintroducing a marriage proposal with Orange? His pleasant attitude toward me lately elicits suspicions."

Mary smiled. "You are quite correct to suspect George of pursuing his own secret battle plans when he is uncharacteristically genteel. If his intention is such, he will find himself opposed by the majority of his family, including his mother."

Charlotte clasped Mary's hands, "Thank you for your support," and she curtseyed slightly. "What do you make of his new wig?"

Her aunt pressed her lips together in thought. "I am not used to seeing a man's own natural hair colour. Anything but white powder is highly unusual. Perhaps my brother is attempting to initiate a new style, bringing the attention of eligible women for his next official wedding."

"And when will you marry, Aunt Mary?"

"That is a good question without a good answer, my Charlotte." She turned her face away so that her niece could not see the tears she blinked away. "I must wait until those ahead of me have been suitably settled. Being the youngest, I have been kept in the back of the royal cupboard awaiting the day I may marry."

"But you're the prettiest of my aunts, if I may say so."

"How kind of you to say, child," and Mary did not disagree with that opinion.

"Have you an eye on anyone?" Charlotte interrogated.

"Why do you ask, dear Charlotte?" her aunt appeared ruffled.

"It is my fondest wish that we do not compete for the hand of the same gentleman."

Mary laughed, "My dear, I am 20 years older than you. I shall most likely be betrothed to some elderly lord or duke for the sake of maintaining our precious bloodline."

"But you seem so young. I would not want to upset you ever."

"I have no interest in the Prussian, Augustus, if that is what you are asking."

Charlotte cast her gaze down, "No, I fear my courting with Augustus is *finis*. It is after another gentleman I inquire."

"Ah, I see. And who is the gentleman you desire to know?"

Charlotte looked left and right as if someone might overhear. "Have you had any interaction with the Prince of Saxe-Coburg?"

"Ernest or Leopold?"

"You know them both?"

Princess Mary laughed, "I have met both of them, yes, but they are night and day, those two. Ernest is too old, too wild and too married to be your man, so I am guessing we shall be discussing the other one, Leopold."

"I don't like him," Charlotte parlayed, "he does not suit my tastes."

"From what I remember of him, he is very good looking, and an excellent officer."

"He has been writing the Prince Regent. Apparently buttering him up so he can request my hand." Charlotte turned away.

"You could do much worse, Charlotte. Remember, they almost had you packed up and crated off to Holland."

"I suppose he is not the worst possible suitor."

"However," and Mary raised an admonishing finger, "His family is rather impoverished and you may not be able to afford the type of stylish life you fancy so."

"That is to be considered as well."

"My dear, you are the most eligible bride in all the world. Pray do not settle for less than what will make you happiest. Keep in mind I shall be foisted off to some old codger for the contentment of the family, not my own."

"I do read Jane Austen," Charlotte confided.

Charlotte: The People's Princess

"Me too!" and they giggled. "However," and her aunt returned to seriousness, "I do agree with my brother, and this Hesse matter must be settled, and the sooner the better. You cannot allow your conniving mother to do anything to usurp your standing."

"Yes, my beautiful, young aunt," she kissed Mary's hand, "the sooner the better!"

5 November 1817, Claremont House, Surrey
Evening

The doctors swarmed around Charlotte's bed. One pointed between her legs and moved a lamp to illuminate the Princess's body.

"Your Highness, I believe I see the baby's head," Sir Richard Croft informed Charlotte. "However, you have not completely dilated. This may take a while, and I'm afraid there might be some more pain."

Prince Leo examined his wife's face, seeing the anguish and anxiety contorting her features, then asked, "Sir Richard, can she not have some brandy to ease the pain?"

"Nothing!" Croft proclaimed without looking up, "Nothing until the baby is delivered."

Baron Stockmar stepped in, "But Croft, you expect she is going to just dilate on her own? Brandy might ease her just enough to allow for relaxation of the cervix."

"Nothing!" Sir Richard repeated. "I have seen lesser women overcome more arduous obstacles. The Princess can do this on her own without assistance. I assure you."

24 December 1815, Warwick House, London
Early afternoon

"I just love your new entryway, dearest Charlotte," proclaimed Miss Margaret Mercer Elphinstone as she gavotted into the drawing room. "So spacious! Who designed it for you? Christopher Wren? Ha, ha, ha."

After discovering the entrance to Warwick House boarded closed, Mercer walked around to Prince George's home, Carlton House. The service staff informed her that Charlotte was no longer allowed to exit at will, and all visitors must pass through Carlton House first. While walking though, she took note of the extravagant Holiday decorations, ribbons, candles, crystal, bowers and statuettes.

"You are divinely funny, Miss M," Charlotte responded sourly from her writing desk. "After my little escapade of July last, Papa saw to it that there was no way in or out of Warwick except directly through Carlton. Dullness visible. A veritable prison! I might as well reside in Newgate," and she held her hands up in front of her face grasping invisible vertical bars.

"And you're no Jack Sheppard, to be sure. At least this keeps the strays and waifs from peddling at your doorstep," she quipped with arched eyebrows.

"Yet one can easily smell them as they pass by," and she pinched at her nose for effect.

"Besides, you have all of bloody London out there instead of sleepy little Weymouth or the dark of Windsor Forest." With the sun low in sky, shadows fell across most of the chamber.

"You're in a joyous good mood today. It is Christmas Eve, after all, but what else has you so impossibly giddy?" Charlotte motioned to a chair beside the desk.

"Aside from a visit with my beloved Count Flahault, I bring you good tidings, distressed damsel." Mercer sat next to her friend.

"And how is your betrothed today? And should I begin preparing for the impending nuptials?" Charlotte lit the candle on the desk.

Mercer waved her hand dismissively, partially due to Charlotte's question and partially due to the smoke, "Horrors! We shan't be married for at least a year hence. Don't have me condemned to unholy matrimony before you, my dear." She glanced back toward Carlton House, "I must say this place is a bit more drab than usual. Especially compared to the decorations of your flamboyant neighbour."

Charlotte pursed her lips and scowled. "Prinny did not give me a Holiday allowance for such frivolous things this year. Father Christmas he is not!"

Mercer smiled and waved her arms, "Anyway and anyhow, my mission here today is to give you hope and cheer!"

"With all the news of death and war from the Continent, it shall be a welcome relief, M. When we heard that the Duke of Brunswick had been killed leading his charge at Quatre Bras, Prinny allowed me to write to mother. I composed a lengthy paean to my uncle, praising his accomplishments and mourning his loss. Mother never wrote back." She glanced down at her hands. "It galls me so. Mercer, pray never tell anyone this, but if I ever ascend the throne, one of my first official acts will be to lock her up in a madhouse."

Margaret's eyes widened to their fullest.

Charlotte looked up, "Oh, don't get me wrong. My head and my heart frequently tell me a different story and lead me widely asunder. I do have very, very strong feelings of affection for the daft old Princess, but at times her behavior angers, horrifies and disgusts me." Charlotte waved her hand as if turning a page in the air. "And, so, a cheerful tale would be most delightful. Do tell!"

"Oh, where to begin? Let's see. Father and I finally met up with your Captain Hesse. He assured us that he had burned all of your letters and showed us the empty storage box."

Charlotte exhaled heavily. "Thank goodness, maybe my father will stop hounding me to marry the Little Frog now for fear that no other man would ever have me. What about my friendship gifts?"

"He gave us some trinkets to return to you but said that the turquoise ring fell off his plume in battle and he has no idea as to the whereabouts of the watch."

"That piece is of little consequence. Now I can start lobbying the Prince Regent about my interest in the Leo." She paused a moment and watched her friend play with the ribbons on her blouse. "Margaret Mercer, would you believe that Mr. Hesse had the nerve to appear in Weymouth while I was out there last month?"

"No! Really?" She gazed up.

"Yes! From my lodge window I spied him pacing along the esplanade–and I had to look twice to make sure it was identically himself. The poor thing had his arm in a sling." She imitated the posture. "When I told the cunning old General about it, he confronted Hesse and instructed him to leave immediately. Mr. H claimed he had no knowledge of my being there and had only stopped for the night on his way out to Cornwall. What balderdash!"

"It might be possible, C. He's not a very good prevaricator, you know."

"That's true, but how upsetting to see him unexpectedly like that," and the Princess glanced down at her folded hands.

"I'm sure it was quite a shock, my dear."

"Not as much as the package Miss Knight dropped in my lap earlier in the year." She lifted her hands and dropped them on her thighs.

Mercer studied her friend's face for a clue without success, "And what was that, my dear C?"

Charlotte adjusted herself in the chair, "Augustus returned the miniature and ring I had given him."

"Well, I think we both knew that was concluded."

"Yes, but it's the letter that came with that shocked me." She jutted her chin and closed her eyes. "So offensive that I burned it immediately."

"Can you remember any of it?"

The Princess waved a hand in the air, "It was piffle about his deep devotion to me that he could never reveal because of strict adherence to his precious military duty. Oh, and listen to this: He felt keeping my portrait would just make things worse for him."

"Regrettable. Another one who is not such a good prevaricator. I pity his next love intrigue."

"I would say that if anything was further wanted to decide this affair, *that* did it. One of my favourite schemes... terminated." She glanced downward.

"I'm sure your family was pleased." She smiled tightly and wrinkled her nose.

Charlotte closed her eyes briefly and opened then again. "Not a one of them favoured Prussia. Most thought he was too old and too impure. It appears I was the only one subject to his obvious charms."

Mercer touched her chin with a finger. "Remember the chat we had after your last birthday when you told me your father was acting suspiciously nice to you?" Charlotte raised her head and nodded. "I haven't had the chance to tell you, but he subsequently summoned the Admiral and myself out to Brighton ostensibly to discuss plans for retrieving the Hesse papers. After a few minutes of strategising, he nonchalantly brought up the topic of Orange."

"Oh, no!" Charlotte looked up at the tattered ceiling.

"Oh, yes! He inquired into our feelings about such a marriage. You and I were quite correct about his false kindness. He still wants to foist you off to the Neverlands." She raised and lowered her eyebrows.

"How horrid! What did you tell him?"

"Father murmured some drivel about how the Prince Regent should have the privilege of determining whom his daughter should marry. I wanted to kick him in the foot!" Charlotte giggled. "Then your father went on about how it would be the only way to save your blotted reputation, get you out of your mother's clutches and make you eternally happy."

"Rubbish!" She shook her head slowly.

"I said, 'Your Highness, I believe it is not actually necessary to marry one man to apologise for writing love letters to another.'" Charlotte put her hand to her mouth. "When he did not respond, I added, 'The last time I spoke to Princess Charlotte, she told me she would rather continue the restraint and deprivations of the last six months at Cranbourne rather than marry the Hereditary Prince of Orange."

The Princess stood and stamped her foot with fists clenched, "I would choose imprisonment in the Tower over a matrimonial connection to the Little Frog!"

She glanced up at Charlotte, "He might very well give you that choice, my dear."

Charlotte: The People's Princess

"I shall have to write him again and make plain that I shall never marry *that* one." She sat down and shifted away from her friend, glancing at an empty hallway.

"Sometimes you worry me, Miss C."

"How so, Miss M?" and she turned to face Mercer.

"You fancy yourself as the heroine of a Miss Jane Austen novel yet to be written. Men are clamouring for your hand from all over Europe. Like sampling food on a sideboard, you taste one and then another. When you are quite finished with them you chew them up or spit them out, ready to move on to the next delightful morsel." She paused briefly, "My fear is that you may do the same with the Leo, after determining that he has faults, as every man does."

The Princess turned her face away, "Not this time, M. Leo is the one. I am certain of it."

"Which is what you said about Thomas and Richard and Harold and Augustus. One could get the idea that you would wed anyone–well, almost anyone–just to get out from under your father's control."

"But Prince Leopold is different!" She turned back, eyes gleaming. "He's a gentleman, soldier..."

"Pauper." She stared directly at Charlotte.

"Perhaps a pauper, but a well-behaved, dignified and sober pauper. At least he has the courage to contact my father directly and negotiate his position, and he has indicated he is saving himself until we can wed."

"That is admirable." Her eyebrows raised. "It sounds like you have your mind set, Lizzy Bennett. You have found your Mr. Darcy."

"And you are so *Emma*." They both grinned. "Do you suppose the Count is your Mr. Knightley?"

"Hardly! His father did not marry my mother." She put a finger to her temple. "Although... I suppose if his mother married my father, it just might work."

"Oh stop!" She smiled. "Your father is quite happy with Hester. You needn't waste your matchmaking skills on anyone but me," and she pointed to herself. "Prinny may want me to marry my Mr. Bingley, but I already have one aunt and one uncle on my side about the good Prince Leopold. Even old Plug-Nose herself let me know that she would prefer it if I refrained from marrying a man I did not like."

Margaret looked quizzically at Charlotte, "Plug-Nose?"

The Princess smiled, "Granny. From her snuff habit."

"I see," her eyes opened widely and her chin elevated slightly. "Are you ready for some words from your Leo?"

Charlotte perked up immediately, "You have heard from him, M?" Her voice elevated in pitch and volume.

Mercer nodded slowly. "I didn't want to start the conversation with this because we most likely would not have discussed anything else at all." She smiled at Charlotte's eagerness. "Shall I begin?"

"Oh, yes, please! Oh, yes!" and she leaned closer to her friend.

"First off, let me say that the post was slowed severely due to all the military hoohah on the Continent. It took up to a month–a MONTH–for letters to get delivered at times, but I have managed to be your attorney, acting in your best interests, of course."

"Of course!" She nodded.

"He first wrote back to me from Vienna indicating he could not think of coming to England because he had to join the Russian army and resume his duties after that Napoleon fellow escaped. However, he did indicate that he would call as soon as possible, if that is acceptable to Your Highness."

"Most acceptable, M! Most acceptable!" She nodded again.

"Well, it is not up to me to communicate so. If your father ever found out I had an active role in arranging your marriage, I fear you and I would never see each other again."

"True, sadly true. But you did write him back?"

"Oh, yes, but I merely *hinted* at your continuing interest in his suit."

"I guess that is better than nothing. No one is more warm or eager about this." She squinted, "If only we could be open in our communications."

"Diplomacy and tact, my dear. Diplomacy and tact." She patted Charlotte's hand. "Just as you have a powerful want of his company due to its absence, let him build up a desire for you so strong that he can no longer live without you by his side." Mercer lifted her chin and glanced sideways. "He will plead his case to Prinny soon enough."

The Princess stared into the empty hallway again, "I suppose you are right, as always."

"No matter, C," and she looked directly at Charlotte, "because I received a post from him only a few days later, most assuredly before he had a chance to read mine, stating he would not want to risk returning to England without an invitation from His Royal Bum Boil. Leo is afraid if he shows up unannounced, your father will pitch him onto the dustheap."

"He is probably correct about that." Charlotte studied Mercer's bland expression and then pounded a fist on her knee. "Why does everything have to be so bloody frustrating?!"

"Ah, the life of a Royal." She glanced skyward and faced her palms up.

"Stop it, Mercer! Pray do not mock," Charlotte pouted.

Margaret looked directly at the Princess with a raised eyebrow, "Sorry, my dearest Charlotte, but we common folk would gladly trade stations."

"All right, all right! I shan't gloom you further."

"But there is some good news, remember?" She smiled with a bit of a squint.

"Pray continue, Good Woman!" She pointed at Mercer as if commanding from the throne.

"Once Leo reached Paris, post resumed and we kept up a regular colloquy. I encouraged him to express his interest. You can read his writings later for I brought them with me," she patted her pocket, "but I think it best not to leave them here where prying eyes could see them."

"Yes, but I so want to see them!" and she tried to get a glimpse.

"Worry not, Princess, you shall have your Prince's wooing. All in good time."

"All the same, I am delighted–nay, charmed–nay, FLATTERED–that the Leo scribes his sentiments and feelings for me. I do hope his writing is acceptable."

"His handwriting is quite clear."

"No, silly, his style!" they both giggled. "I hope he studied Shakespeare and not Milton."

"You shall soon see for yourself." She patted her pocket once again.

"I don't know how to thank you enough for your service, Countess Flahault de la Billarderie. Preach up prudence! *We* give you *carte blanche* to represent *our* feelings and desires to His Serene Highness, Prince Leopold." She held out her hands to Mercer, who did not take them. "I suppose it is for the best that you retain his letters until we see each other again. That way, no one can accuse you of forwarding his writings to me. Oh, this is all so foolish!" Charlotte raised her hands over her head then dropped them into her lap. "How can I ever begin to repay you, my dearest Margaret Mercer?"

"My dearest Charlotte Augusta, please refrain from titling me Countess until after the wedding. Until then, Baroness Keith should suffice." They touched hands and laughed. "By the way, I have to admit I am getting rather peckish. Can we ring for supper? You can peruse Leo's poetry whilst I fill my gullet!"

The Princess could not reach for the bell quickly enough.

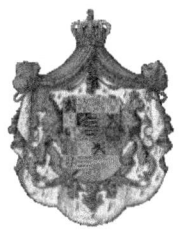

5 November 1817, Claremont House, Surrey
Evening

Sir Richard Croft looked up from Charlotte's body. He stood and approached Stockmar standing in the corner. "Baron Stockmar, the baby is turned and it is not the head we see," he whispered.

"How do you suggest we continue, Sir Richard? You have much more experience in this area than I."

"First off," Croft confided, "I do not wish to alarm their Highnesses any further. If we can manipulate the Princess's abdomen without arousing suspicion, we may be able to maneuver the baby into proper position."

"A good plan," and Stockmar glanced over at the drowsy couple. "Perhaps we could announce that you are palpating to determine the progress, all the while you are applying pressure in the proper areas to align the infant."

"Well done, Baron. If we cannot position the baby correctly, the Princess will not be able to expel it herself."

"Due to weakness brought about by deprivation, Sir Richard?"

Croft glowered at Stockmar.

7 January 1816, Brighton Pavilion
Evening

Candle lanterns placed in the beach sand beside the pavilion spelled out:

Hail Princess Charlotte

Europe's Hope and Britain's Glory

"This place is magnificent!" Charlotte raised her arms and twirled around the grand room, gazing up at all the Asian-styled decor. Vases from India, silks from China and teak trim panels flourished beneath the sky blue rotunda and lotus petal chandeliers. "I just wish His Royal Highness had allowed me to see the pavilion sooner. It is an amazing structure! This will be the best birthday ever!"

Her grandmother smiled tightly. Even though it was only relatives at the party, Charlotte appreciated not spending her birthday virtually alone, as she had the last few years.

Mr. Louis selected for the Princess a light-yellow frock with pearl beading and a farthingale skirt. Brussels lace trim adorned the bodice and hem. The King Charles I sapphire dangled around her fair neck. Golden brown ringlets cascaded from her hair along the side of her wide face.

The main dining table occupied the middle of the room. Along the inside wall, below the immense tapestries showing elephants and Hindu gods, were small tables with bowls of nuts, plates of finger sandwiches and pitchers of wine.

Prince George entered with entourage and made his way to the Merlin chair. "Where is the birthday girl?" He rotated the wheels slightly with his hands so that the chair turned left then right.

"Here, Papa!"

"Step forward and approach."

Charlotte moved to her father's chaise, admiring the ornate wall hangings while receiving hugs and kisses from her aunts and uncles along the way. In front of the Prince Regent, she curtseyed low and respectfully. She assumed her standard pose with hands clasped behind, thrusting her waist forward.

George arranged his carcass in the chaise and then stared at his daughter for a few seconds. No one spoke.

"Princess Charlotte Augusta of Wales," he addressed the entire hall, "when did you grow to be such a beautiful young lady?" The father now looked at the daughter with a man's eyes. "You are too radiant for spinsterhood," some of Charlotte's unmarried aunts took umbrage, "You should be married and carry on the Guelph of Hanover lineage. A princess of your age who has not yet wed is almost certainly destined to be an old maid." He laughed at his joke and the rest of the guests joined in, except for the unmarried aunts.

"I would have wed, Your Highness, but you and I disagreed on the groom." A few people chuckled.

"We have disagreed, that is quite correct. The Prince Regent has looked to the West and you to the East. Opposite directions, as it were."

"Yes, Papa," and she made a slight curtsey.

"However, the time has come to insist on your marriage to a suitable groom of Our choosing."

"But Papa…"

"Pray let me finish, dear daughter," he pointed a finger up to the ceiling and cocked his head slightly, "We are pontificating." The crowd laughed with the Prince.

"Yes, Your Highness," Charlotte demurred with another curtsey.

The Prince looked about the hall, observing his family and the staff. "We have received some rather unfortunate news from the low, little country of Holland that the Hereditary Prince of Orange is now engaged to the Grand Duchess Anne, youngest sister of Tsar Alexander, thus removing him from the pool of eligible suitors for our young Princess."

Charlotte smiled so hard her cheeks hurt. Candlelight radiated off the pearl beads in sympathy with her relief.

"After much deliberation, and wise counsel from some of the esteemed Royal siblings," he paused to look at his assembled family and friends, "We have chosen a man who has impressed us with his valour, courage and leadership. A man from noble ancestors, a man with vast military experience, a man who assisted Wellington in defeating Napoleon, a man who will provide guidance to the Princess of Wales when it is her time to lead this mighty nation… but not for many years to come." A few people in the crowd chuckled. "We have sent a letter of invitation and expect his presence within the month."

This apostrophe had Charlotte worried that her family had chosen some old military man for her. Who could it possibly be?

"Charlotte Augusta, the bridegroom We have chosen for you is…" he paused for effect, glancing about the room, "His Serene Highness, Prince Leopold George Frederick of Saxe-Coburg."

Charlotte: The People's Princess

The Princess stepped forward, broke protocol and hugged her father as the crowd cheered and applauded. George grunted and unintentionally passed wind.

"Thank you, Papa, Your Highness. This *is* the best birthday ever!" Charlotte kissed her father for the first time.

As she released the hug, her father said for her ears alone, "Don't thank Us. Your dear friend Duchess Caroline arranged the Orange marriage through her surreptitious manipulations. Her intention all along was to join the Dutch forces with those of Russia." Charlotte stiffened and her eyes blazed. "She wanted England out of the way, and you played right into her hands. We warned you about that woman, but We shall see who emerges victorious."

The Princess took a step back, "I see. People have warned me that others will attempt to take advantage of my station." *Espérance et constance,* she mused as George nodded his globular head rhythmically. Charlotte thought about her prince and smiled. "When does Leopold arrive, Papa?"

"The courier has had some difficulty locating him. Once he left Paris, his whereabouts have been virtually unknown. Fret not, We shall find him. Now, go thank your aunts and uncles, for it is they who convinced Us to allow you to choose. Then, perhaps you should thank Miss Jane Austen as well."

Charlotte put her hand out to touch her father, but he pulled away instinctively. "Papa, I am surprised you even know about Jane Austen."

"My dearest Charlotte," the Prince droned, "that Austen woman has caused me more aggravation than I care to think about!" He exhaled loudly. "The suggestion, the very *idea*, that women can be the equal of men is preposterous!" The Prince pointed toward Heaven.

"Preposterous!" Charlotte repeated, also pointing skyward.

George examined his daughter again with wary eyes, "Go enjoy your party, Charlotte," and he pointed toward the centre of the room.

"Thank you again, father," she smiled, "Thank you, thank you, thank you." She hurried over to her aunts.

The Prince Regent watched as she flounced away, hoping he had made the proper decision.

5 November 1817, Claremont House, Surrey
Evening

Baron Stockmar opened the door to the darkened hallway and motioned to Leopold to follow him. Once they were both out of the bedchamber, he closed the door behind them. Only a few lights had been lit and shadows flickered on the walls and floor.

"Leo, the news is not good," Stockmar whispered as he led the Prince farther away from Charlotte. "Croft tells me he felt no movement, and we fear the baby is stillborn. I am truly sorry, my friend."

Leopold sopped at his moist brow with a cloth. "Thank you, Stocky. Charlotte and I are prepared for the worst. We had already discussed this terrible possibility." He attempted to smile but could not. He looked into Stockmar's eyes, "After she recovers from this tragedy, we will make every attempt to produce a proper heir."

The Baron hugged his friend. "So wise for one so young. Shall we rejoin the rest of the party and break the news to Charlotte?"

Prince Leopold nodded weakly and followed his friend back to the Princess's chamber. Stockmar opened the door and led them back into the room.

Charlotte turned to look when she heard them enter. Profuse sweating hid the tears. Her face seemed sunken, lifeless. Defeated eyes focused on Leopold. He held her gaze as best he could while tears clouded his own vision.

Charlotte: The People's Princess

Carlton House decorated for the
Wedding of Charlotte and Leopold

2 May 1816, Queen's House (Buckingham), London
Evening

"Louise, look at the size of the crowd!" Charlotte held the red brocade curtain back as she peered out the second-story bedchamber window. She gazed out over the small park at a wave of onlookers undulating around the entrance to the manor.

"My Princess, they all want to see you on your wedding. Now, please come back so that I can finish dressing you."

Charlotte had dined with her grandmother and was getting ready to marry Prince Leopold.

"Yes, Mrs. Louis." She dropped the drapery and walked over to her dresser. "I can't believe the day is finally here! Between Papa being ill with his gout and Leopold being ill with rheumatism, we have had to postpone so many times."

"When we see each other next, you will be Mrs. Leopold." Louise undid the Princess's day gown being careful not to entangle the dangling bejeweled earrings.

Charlotte stepped out of her dinner clothes maintaining the diamond necklace against her chest. "I shall remain Princess Charlotte of Wales, but I will also be the wife of His Serene Highness, Prince Leopold George Christian Frederick of Saxe-Coburg."

"So many names for so little money." Mrs. Louis began dressing Charlotte in the undergarments, slipping one arm and then the other through the sleeve holes. "Is it not the duty of the bridegroom to provide a purse for his beloved?" She buttoned the dainty fabric fastidiously.

The Princess looked down on the dresser as she began to wrap the Brussels lace slip around Charlotte, "You know I'm not marrying him for his fortune."

The dresser fastened the garment and spoke without looking up, "My dear Princess, everyone knows that! *Tout le monde!*"

"I must admit it is going to be difficult to remain serious when we get to the part where he promises to endow me with all his worldly goods." She glanced upward at the decorative ceiling molding. "It was terribly wrong of me, but when the Archbishop went over the ceremony earlier, I broke out in giggles at that point. He may not possess any wealth, but Leopold is the dearest man to my heart there ever was."

Mrs. Louis carried the silver lamé and silk dress, ready to encase the Princess in it. "He is a good man, my Charlotte, and the best man for you. *Si vous plait*, lift your arms, dear." She lowered the embroidered dress over the Princess.

"I certainly hope so, Louise. I have fought dearly for this. Mercer had her doubts that I would even follow through to completion."

The dresser began to fit the Princess into the dress, "And where is your Miss Elphinstone? She should be here."

"Oh, Louise, I am afraid she is protesting this evening. She sent a message earlier saying she did not feel well, but that is no excuse to miss the wedding of your best friend." Mrs. Louis pulled the fabric tightly and closed a button with some effort. "Oooof!"

"*Mais, non!* What do you think happened?" She struggled to get another button through a loop.

"Aaaaggghh!" Charlotte uttered. "I believe it is dear Leopold's fault. He did not like Mercer's choice of fiancé. It seems the two men competed for the attention of the same woman in Paris, and the other fellow, a Count, ended up winning the grand prize."

"But you got your *grand prix, oui*?" She closed another button.

"*Mais, oui!* Leopold has turned out to be so much more wonderful than I had ever hoped. Thank goodness Hortense chose the other fellow, but Leopold is still bitter and warned Mercer to be wary of the Count."

"That is still no reason to miss your wedding. Everyone else in all of England would want to be here." Louise stepped back to eyeball the gown. "She has not chose wisely."

"*Merci*, Louise. I agree."

"Look at you, *ma chère! Régardez!* You are so beautiful in this dress."

"I guess." She looked down at it with a hint of blasé. "Grandmama chose this. I don't know if I would have wanted all these shells." She pointed out the various adornments. "The flowers are pretty enough, though." She looked up and turned her torso to face behind her. "And this train!" Charlotte hefted a portion in her hand. "It is longer than I am tall. Thank goodness I am not expected to carry it myself." She dropped the fabric and faced front.

"*Oui!* Thank goodness indeed." Mrs. Louis continued to touch and adjust the dress.

"I can't believe the good taste Papa had in jewelry. He gave me these earrings and necklace." She touched the baubles lightly.

"So many diamonds! What about the bracelet?"

"Oh, Leopold gave me that." While not as ornate as the other jewelry, it still had diamonds. She grasped it tightly. "He is so sweet. I feel very, very lucky."

"And you should, *ma princesse*." Mrs. Louis finished adjusting the outfit. "Pardon my asking, *Mademoiselle*, but I will be staying on with you, yes?"

"Of course, Louise!" She hugged the woman, "I want no other person to dress me."

The dresser picked up Charlotte's gloves. "And where will we live, if I may ask?"

"Prinny has purchased a home in Surrey for us, Claremont, I believe. You will love it." She held out her hands as Louise began putting the lace gloves on her.

"I will love it if I can continue with you, yes. Who lived there before?"

"Uncle Frederick and Aunt Frederica showed it to me when I was staying with them at Oatlands a while back. I thought it was the most beautiful place possible." She held up the one gloved hand and examined the lace. "Fortunately for me, but unfortunately for the previous owner, his wife died in childbirth–poor thing–and he decided to sell it."

"Will you not miss London?"

"Oh, Louise," and she pulled her hand back, "Prinny also gave us this pathetic little hovel in Park Lane. It is dark and small, and it might do for the season, but we shall seriously have to find something better." Charlotte adjusted the fingers of the gloves.

"And where will you spend *la lune de miel?* Are you going abroad?"

"Not just yet." The Princess turned and studied herself in the mirror. "Uncle Frederick is giving us Oatlands. He has been so good to us. And you are coming with me, dear Louise."

"*Vraiment?* On your honeymoon?" the dresser inquired with surprise.

"*D'accord.*" One hand flopped over, palm up. "With all my outfits, I wouldn't know where to begin. I must have you along," and she brought the hand up to her chest.

"*Merci mille fois, ma chère Princesse.*" She turned and glanced at the mantel clock. "Charlotte, look at the time! It is almost half past eight. We must have you ready soon."

"It is not that far, and I could have walked the Mall to get to Carlton."

"But, *ma chère*, the people want to see you ride in a coach, and do you think you could walk very far in that dress?" She indicated the lengthy train.

"I suppose you're right." Charlotte dropped her hands to her sides and looked directly at Mrs. Louis, "Louise, am I doing the right thing? Marrying Leopold, I mean."

Mrs. Louis stared back at her. "*Ma chère*, I have known you a very long time, since you were small." She picked up the diamond-encrusted headpiece shaped like roses and leaves. "Every bride is nervous before her marriage. Many years ago the nervous came because you did not know your husband, you meet him on your wedding day." She paused in reflection of her own arranged marriage. "Today, the young women have the nervous because they are marrying the man they want to be with. They wonder if they are doing the right thing, as you say." She placed the jeweled wreath on Charlotte's head.

The bride stood in silence waiting for her dresser to continue.

"I am happy for you that you stop to consider whether you are doing this right thing. It shows you have–how your Mrs. Austen puts it–sensibility."

The Princess cast her gaze downward.

"Charlotte, go you and marry your prince. Become the princess you always wanted to be. Prepare to have the throne of your father someday."

At that, Charlotte looked up.

"Are you doing the right thing?" Mrs. Louis shrugged. "Who can say, but I will tell you this, Princess Charlotte Augusta of Wales: not marrying Prince Leopold would definitely be the wrong thing." She smiled and winked at Charlotte.

Charlotte smiled back and held her head with nobility.

Charlotte: The People's Princess

Let every Briton raise his voice,
Let every British heart rejoice,
 On this auspicious day;
For soon shall England's Hope entwine
The Brunswick with the Saxon line,
 In Hymen's hallow'd ray.

Illustrious pair! May Mercy sway
The sceptre of these realms to-day,
 O may she brightly shine;
May Gratitude be taught to raise
To Brunswick's House the hymn of praise
 And hail that mercy thine.

May each poor prisoner in his cell,
With rapture of thy marriage tell,
 May each to-day be free;
Joy will the grateful mandate take
And Heaven will bless for Mercy's sake,
 And hallow the decree.

Through life's short round we'll merry raise
To England's Hope, the hymn of praise,
 And hail thy wedding day;
O then, let Mercy brightly shine,
Let her with Joy this day entwine,
 To shed a heavenly ray.

—Anonymous, written at Weymouth for the Royal Couple

5 November 1817, Claremont House, Surrey
Evening

Sir Richard had been examining Charlotte for a few minutes when Leopold and Stockmar re-entered the chamber. He looked up, "Baron Stockmar, I believe the Princess has now dilated sufficiently for parturition." He turned his attention to Charlotte again.

"*With no thanks to you,*" thought Stockmar, who, by this point had grown impatient with Croft's pompous style and patently inept handling of Charlotte's health. "*Who starves a delivering mother and then expects the poor thing to pop out a baby for your convenience?*"

The Baron looked at Charlotte and wondered what torture would be next. "Thank you, Sir Richard," he said aloud. "How do we proceed?"

Croft kept his focus on Charlotte but spoke loudly, "We encourage the mother to push the baby through the birth canal. That is how we proceed."

The Prince looked at Stockmar with an unspoken question. Stockmar looked at Charlotte, pale, bloated, gasping and exhausted. "Sir Richard, I believe that Charlotte does not possess sufficient strength for birth. You have deprived her of all nutrition for three days."

Charlotte: The People's Princess

The accoucher slowly rotated his head to face the Baron, "Sir, I am given the royal charge here. If you do not agree with my modern, scientific methods, then I suggest you remove yourself at once!"

"Please, gentlemen," Leopold whimpered. "Charlotte is weak enough without your arguments." He clasped her withered hand.

"Yes, Croft, you are in charge here," Stockmar continued, "and shall be responsible for whatever happens, for good or for bad. Your inept mishandling of this baby and its mother will not go unnoticed!"

"Enough of your slanderous attacks, sir!" Sir Richard responded. "Please leave at once!" He pointed to the door.

"Or what, Sir Richard?" Stockmar challenged with his hands on his hips.

"Please stop!" Leopold begged, "The both of—"

"AAaaaggggghhhhh!!!" Charlotte screamed and all heads turned to see the movement of her abdomen as the large bulge began moving toward her legs.

Britain's Glory

4 August 1816, Kensington Palace, London
Evening

"These apartments are marvelous, Charlotte!" Mercer exclaimed as she entered the new home of the Princess and Prince. A high, white ceiling lorded over the parqueted wooden floor. The walls were also white with gold-trim square columns every six feet. Some of the panels had mirrors, giving the room the appearance of being much wider. "So superior to Warwick."

Charlotte approached her friend and stated, "Anything is better than Warwick," then recanted, "Except Camelford. That was dreadfully horrid." She touched Mercer's hand, "It's a good thing you never saw the place. You would like my father even less."

"I don't know that I could like your father less, Princess." They laughed together as Charlotte guided her guest into the apartment. "How did you manage to acquire these spacious rooms? Did someone die?"

"No, nothing so *dramatique*," she flapped her hand. "Uncle Frederick, who has been so good to me, offered us his rooms because he is no longer using them. Once Leopold and I finally decided Camelford was impossible, Cumberland House seemed the best candidate, but repairs would have been excessive. We looked at half a dozen other places, all worse than Camelford–if you can believe–and both of us agreed uncle's Kensington apartment was the right place."

"Well done! You have done well, my dear C. Oh my! May I still call you that or must we all address you as Your Royal Highness now?"

"Miss M, stop being silly!" and she flapped her hand again. "You may call me as you wish. You are my oldest and dearest friend."

Candlelight from the wall sconces flickered on the pair as they strutted through the hall toward the sitting room.

"Tell me, though," she placed a finger to the corner of her mouth, "when you eventually ascend to the throne, will you want to wear a periwig to indicate just how high your royalness rises?"

"Mercer! That presumes the death of my grandfather and father. How dare we address such a topic so prematurely!" Charlotte straightened her back. "Yes, I do believe a periwig would be in order... someday...," she fingered a lock of her own hair.

"Well, my someday sovereign, when I wed Flahault next season, you shall henceforth properly address me as Baroness," and she posed haughtily for effect.

"Yes, your Baroness-ship," as Charlotte bowed mockingly to her friend. "So tell me all about Scotland. I've only heard of it through Shakespeare."

"Oh, you can't imagine, C," and she sat in a nearby chair. Charlotte quickly followed. "The weather is horrible. Horrible! If it isn't cold and rainy, it's cold and foggy. The days warm enough to walk about are fewer than the fingers on your hands. But I love my Flahault, and I will learn to love my Scotland as well. There must be something there that the bloody Scots kept fighting for all those years."

"And the Baron?"

"He manages to be away much of the time hunting, foxing, killing little things, but if that is what makes him happy, I am loath to interfere. At least until after the wedding," and Mercer broke out in pearls of laughter, but Charlotte kept still, thinking about her friend avoiding her own wedding. "He is quite the dashing character when he graces me with his presence: dancing, singing, mask balls. Quite festive, actually. Almost on par with this dreary old town."

"No wonder you did not return for your birthday this year. I would have thought the lack of adequate entertainments would have driven you mad."

"Perhaps we don't have the theatres, such as those you and the Leo attend." Charlotte perked up and looked directly at

Mercer. "Yes, the news of your evenings reaches the provinces. However, we must make due with only the strapping hunks of men that constantly attend us."

"Oh my!"

"That kilt *is* a clever garment," she winked at her friend. "So tell me of your adventures. I am dieing to hear!"

"My goodness," Charlotte began, "it has been such a long while. Well, for a start, Prinny surprised us with a visit while we were at Oatlands."

"Oh, no."

"Oh, yes! He bored us silly for over two hours–two HOURS–on military costumes of various nations. The cut of such and such a coat, a cape, the sleeve, even the small clothes! Can you believe?" she flapped a hand again. "On our honeymoon! Other than that he was uncharacteristically pleasant and in good humour."

"Perhaps he has a new mistress in Weymouth."

"Ugh, I don't even want to think of such things! Ew!" Charlotte wrinkled her nose. "I have met Leopold's best friend, almost like a parallel of you and I, the Baron Christian Stockmar–"

"Oh, another Baron?"

"Yes, and I'm calling him 'Stocky.' He is also a doctor," she bragged.

"How fortunate. Will he be attending you?"

"Unfortunately, no. Papa wants me to see his physician, Baillie."

"Good Old Baillie," Mercer punched the air with her fist. "Is he barrister at the bar as well?"

"Old Baillie, Old Bailey. Very good, M." she shuffled slightly in her chair. "Upon returning to London, we had to endure a long procession of loyal addresses from every local politician possible: the Lord Mayor, of course–"

"Oh, of course."

"–the whole City Council, one at a time, and the leader of every guild imaginable," she bobbed her head side to side as if counting off the visitors. "Both houses of Parliament as well. It seemed interminable."

"Sounds positively dreary."

"And then the whole Hanover dynasty made its way to Camelford, and we had to entertain a hoard of guests in that Lilliputian hovel. If only we could have had them here," and she waved an arm around the spacious room, indicating various paintings and statues.

Mercer stared directly at Charlotte and said, "I remember a young woman whose credo was '*Espérance et constance.*' I wonder what ever happened to her...?"

"All right, Miss M. Point taken," and she looked down at her lap.

"And we curious folk wish to know if you have yet chosen a pet name for your Prince," Mercer pressed.

Charlotte looked up, "*Doucement*," she declared, and her friend merely stared back blankly. "I call him *Doucement*."

"How... sweet. And wherefore do you refer to your husband as a French adverb?"

"Because, dear M, Leopold fancies himself my deportment instructor, and he believes I present myself a bit too strongly at times." She glanced off toward the hallway and blinked with raised eyebrows.

"Maybe just a little bit," Margaret mocked, "but nothing I imagine a German would ever notice."

Charlotte faced Mercer again, "So he coaches me by saying, '*Doucement, ma chère, Doucement,*' whenever I broach his tolerance threshold. He desires me to exhibit the epitome of British princess behavior."

"How utterly dreadful." Mercer sat at attention. "And are you teaching him our mother tongue in return?"

"As a matter of fact I am."

"It sounds like you instruct him on the manners of the English language and he instructs you on the language of the English manners."

"Mercer, you are being terribly rude!" She pointed a finger. "Now, do you want to hear about the theatre or not?"

"Yes, please, Your Royal-ness-ship!" She glanced about, "But would it be possible to have some refreshments during the performance?"

Charlotte touched a hand to her forehead, "How silly of me. Of course." She rang a small bell from the table next to her chair. A middle-aged wiry woman appeared from the door arch and bowed slightly. "Elizabeth, could you bring some tea and biscuits? Thank you." The servant bowed again and disappeared through the arch.

"Thank you, Your Highness," Mercer saluted melodramatically and then relaxed in her chair. "Pray proceed with your theatrical review."

"Well, the first thing we attended was *Bertram* in Drury Lane with that dreamy Edmund Kean."

"He's so-so. So *dra-ma-tique*," she gesticulated with each syllable.

"He's the best. Well, anyway, we arrived late because we had stopped to thank Aunt Frederica for lending us Oatlands." She pointed toward the southwest. "The performance was well into the first act and I feared we would disturb the actors. As we went to sit down, the audience began hissing, and the players stopped cold. I was so embarrassed!" She put a hand up to her face. "Then people started shouting 'Stage Box! Stage Box!' and Leopold–who had never attended the theatre in London–thought they were reprimanding us for disturbing the action."

"Oh my!"

"When I told him what they were after, we moved our seats to the rail and leaned over a bit." She pantomimed moving her chair. "He had never heard of such a thing."

"We do love our Royals." She described descending circles with her hand.

"Yes. At first we were a bit uncomfortable, with people turning their heads to look at us instead of the stage," Charlotte imitated the head movements, "but eventually we relaxed and Leopold even put his arm around me."

"How bold your Prince is! Practically undressing you in public." She pretended to undo her blouse.

"But wait! The following week Prinny gave us his Covent Garden box for *The Jealous Wife*, and at the curtain, the entire cast and crew stood onstage and sang 'God Save the King' with lyrics just for us!"

"How special. Can you remember any of it?"

"That was quite a while back," she glanced up at the ceiling as if the words were printed above her, "but they sang 'Charlotte the Bride' instead of 'God Save the King.'"

"Positively blasphemous! Good thing your grandfather wasn't there to hear it." Mercer shifted a bit in her chair.

The servant returned with a plate of cookies and a polished silver tea set on a cart. She poured two cups, bowed politely and left again.

Mercer started to reach for a cookie, but stopped when she realised it would be better to wait for the Princess. Charlotte observed this and smiled briefly. She waited a few seconds and then picked up a cookie from the plate.

"Pardon my curiosity, Princess, but can your Leo follow the dialogue? Have his language skills improved sufficiently?" She waited until Charlotte's hand was clear of the cart to take her teacup.

"Believe me, you're not the first to inquire so. Most unenlightened people suspect him of being some kind of foreign agent." She nibbled on the cookie even though she wanted to swallow the entire thing at once.

"They shall learn in time."

"I should certainly hope so." She swallowed the remainder in one gulp. "In the meantime, I receive a copy of the script for each play we are going to attend so that I may explain the words to him."

Mercer smiled blandly as she sipped the tea.

"We then had the fortune of seeing the supreme Sarah Siddons play Queen Catherine in *Henry VIII*." She reached for the remaining teacup.

"Wasn't he your great-great-great grandfather or something like that?"

"Umm, I think there would have to be a few more 'great-greats' in there." Charlotte tested the water temperature with a fingertip.

"No one ever wrote a play about my great ancestors, I tell you!" and she drained the rest of the cup.

"I thought you said you were a direct descendant of Lear, or was that Cymbeline...?" She touched her lips to the cup and drew some tea.

"Ha, ha. Maybe someone will write a play about you someday. We could call it *The Preposterous Princess of Pr... Preston and her Pretentious Prince*."

"Leopold is not pretentious!"

"And you're not preposterous?"

The two women held their cups and looked in opposite directions.

Margaret broke the silence after a few seconds, "What have you heard from your dear mama?"

"Not a note, M." She turned to face her friend again, "And Papa is stepping up his noises about a divorce, claiming she has been having adulterous intercourse with foreigners."

"That sounds like a delightful way to travel."

Charlotte turned red, "Margaret Mercer Elphinstone! If my father divorces my mother, weds proper and produces a son, there goes my claim to the throne!"

"Well, we wouldn't want *that*." She set the empty cup on the tray.

"No, We wouldn't!" Charlotte slammed her hand on the table.

"*Doucement, ma chère, Doucement,*" cooed Mercer as she lifted a cookie to her lips.

The Princess inhaled and exhaled heavily. "You are so right, *mon amie*. But talking about the Prince Regent upsets me so." She faced Mercer directly. "I even heard that people have thrown stones at his carriage as it passes."

"Oh, my," hand to mouth, eyelids fluttering.

"Even Miss Jane Austen herself has written a letter to *The Times*." Charlotte picked up a folded newspaper from the table. "Here it is: 'Poor woman,'–referring to my mother–'I shall support her as long as I can, because she is a woman, and because I hate her husband so much. But if I must give up the Princess, I am resolved at least always to think that she would have been respectable, if the Prince had only behaved tolerably by her at first.'" She placed the paper back on the table. "Even Miss Austen detests my father!"

"I would believe anything I heard about Prinny," she grinned, "Particularly if it was false" and continued to chew daintily on the cookie.

Charlotte finished her tea and returned the cup to the tray. "Margaret, we recently attended the opera–and you know I love opera," her friend nodded, "but I took ill during the performance and we had to leave."

Mercer cocked her head slightly, "I believe I read that in the Edinburgh paper. They said you caught a cold or some such silly nonsense." She finished the cookie and brushed her hands. "What really happened?"

Charlotte looked down at her shoes, "Dr. Baillie believes I had a miscarriage."

"Oh, Charlotte, I am so sorry." She reached over to touch her friend, but the Princess drew back. "I know you two want children as soon as possible." Margaret pulled her hand away.

The air in the room suddenly chilled.

"It could be all the excitement affected me so." She looked up, "We shall try again. And again if necessary," she smiled.

Charlotte: The People's Princess

Charlotte and Leopold
at the Opera

"God Save the King"　　　God save our gracious King,
 (original lyrics)　　　　　Long live our noble king,
　　　　　　　　　　　　　God save the king:
　　　　　　　　　　　　　Send him victorious,
　　　　　　　　　　　　　Happy and glorious,
　　　　　　　　　　　　　Long to reign over us:
　　　　　　　　　　　　　God save the King.

 (as sung by theatre players)　Long may the Noble Line,
　　　　　　　　　　　　　When she descended, shine
　　　　　　　　　　　　　In Charlotte the Bride!
　　　　　　　　　　　　　Grant it perpetuate
　　　　　　　　　　　　　And ever make it great;
　　　　　　　　　　　　　On Leopold's blessing wait
　　　　　　　　　　　　　And Charlotte his Bride.

5 November 1817, Claremont House, Surrey
Evening

Sir Richard Croft stood holding the purple-grey stillborn boy, the shriveled blackish umbilical cord still attached. Tears blurred his vision and blinking could not restore his sight.

He had begged, urged, implored and entreated his patient to expel the fetus. Privately, he prayed for an end to this horrible situation with a good outcome for all, especially himself. The mother had groaned and strained, pushed and contorted, all the while claiming to have no more strength. He attempted to massage her swollen belly and encourage the outward movement of the baby. Finally it passed completely through the cervix, whooshing out the birth canal and rested in his bloodied hands.

Gripping the inanimate heir to the British throne, Sir Richard anticipated this was the end of his career, the end of his dream to become Physician Royal, the end of his credibility as a medical authority. All slipping away, away. His perseverations froze him.

Charlotte lay on her back exhausted, sweat-drenched under blood-soaked bedclothes. Leopold gently held her pale wrist. Her irregular breathing included frequent gasps. With what little energy she had left, her head turned toward her vigilant husband, her eyes closed. He looked across at Stockmar.

"For the love of... Croft!" screamed the Baron. "Initiate resuscitation!"

The accoucheur snapped back to the current reality, placed the infant gently on the bed between its mother's legs and began pressing the chest of the dead boy with his trembling fingertips in hopes of the baby breathing on its own. He started gently at first, accelerating in tempo until it matched the racing beats of his own fear-drenched heart.

24 December 1816, Brighton Pavilion
Evening

Charlotte led Leopold into the empty ballroom. "See, as I have told you. No one else is yet here."

Leopold looked about, "It is no... wonder. Your father keeps all of his... guests until the time of dinner separate."

"It makes no sense to me for the family to gather at Yuletide and not be together."

He looked at her and smiled, "And we are together, you and I, that is the important thing."

She hugged him, "Yes, Your Highness is so wise."

Leopold then turned to look at the pine tree which had been brought inside for the evening. "Please, my treasure, assist me to finish the tree decorations," and he walked toward the corner with the lone tree.

Charlotte followed, eying the little green pine. "Why are we doing this, Leopold?"

As he began to attach small crystals and porcelain ornaments to the branches he answered, "It is an old family... custom at

Christmas time. A *Tannenbaum*." He then started to place coloured candles at the ends of some of the branches.

"A curious tradition, indeed," boomed the Prince Regent as he rolled into the room in his Merlin chair. "You kill an innocent tree, drag it into your household, hide its natural beauty with knickknacks, and then set fire to the whole thing. Would it not serve the greater good as hearth kindling?" and he laughed loudly. A few of the other guests who had arrived with him chuckled along.

Leopold turned to face his father-in-law, "Your Highness, if my gesture of goodwill displeases you, I shall remove it at once."

Prince George laughed ever louder, "My boy, the tree may stay. We command it!" Applause trickled up from the onlookers. "The German woman who bore Us also follows this amusing ritual. We are quite inured to it." He rolled off to speak with other guests.

"What means 'inured'?" Leopold inquired of Charlotte.

She glanced up at the overly-decorated ceiling for help. Finding none, "It means being exposed to something you don't like over and over until you finally stop detesting it."

"Ah, *gehärtetes*. Much like the way you feel regarding your Grandmama."

"Exactly so!" and she grabbed his right hand with both of hers and led him to the dinner table.

Their assigned seats were almost at the other end from the Prince Regent. During the holiday goose dinner, Charlotte and Leopold made polite conversation with the various lords and ladies seated near them, even though they had not met the other guests before.

At one point she turned to her husband, "I do believe that Papa has banished us to the farthest reaches as some sort of punishment."

"My treasure," Leopold whispered, "I choose to believe he has trusted us to be his representatives at the other end of the world."

Charlotte kissed his cheek, "*Mein Lieb,* you are such the diplomat. That must be why I love you so. Truly, you are the best husband in all five quarters of this Earth!"

From the other end of the table, a rhythmic banging started slowly and quietly, accelerating and growing louder. Some people used silverware, others used their fist.

Leopold turned to his wife, "Charlotte, what is that noise?"

Her eyes rolled to the tops of their sockets. "Oh, no. His Royal Annoyance is going to speak." They both turned to face the Prince as he squirmed out of his wheeled chair to stand.

"Happy Christmas, everyone!" George roared as if he were Father Christmas himself.

People at the table shouted, "Happy Christmas!" in response.

"As you may have noticed," the Prince Regent continued, "there is a wilting nosegay in the corner," and he indicated Leopold's tree. "My new son-in-law has graced us with the accursed custom of his Germanic people, chopping up an otherwise fine tree, stanchioning it, bedecking it with gewgaws, and then setting it ablaze." A few guests murmured or raised their brows. "Our own Germanic mother, also known as Her Royal Majesty, Queen Charlotte, introduced this festive curiosity to us many years ago, but we had never put her displays in a public area for fear of rabid deportation." He looked about, then laughed. "We give to you *die Weihnachtenbaum*, the tree of Christmas, and Prince Leopold of Saxe-Coburg." He bowed ever so slightly, and the other guests began applauding politely.

"Does that mean he approves?" Leopold asked as he raised his glass returning the salute.

Charlotte shrugged her shoulders twice. "One can never know the mind of Prinny. Just be thankful he took notice, and, pray, do not be upset if your tree has been removed in the morning."

Leopold lowered his eyes.

"During our delightful dinner, the request arose to have Leopold's bride, oh, what's her name...?" The crowd laughed out loud at his joke. "Char-something, entertain us upon the pianoforte." Applause erupted. "Daughter dearest, We command thee to play something for us." More applause rang out as the Prince Regent indicated the nearby keyboard with a wave of his hand.

"Entertainment he wants, does he?" Charlotte grumbled. "I shall give him something to remember." She pushed her chair back with a scrape and started to stand.

Leopold placed his hand lightly on hers. "*Doucement, ma chère, Doucement,*"

"*Doucement,* my bum!" and she marched to the piano in rhythm with the applause.

"Unaccustomed as I am to performing in public," she announced, and a few laughs interrupted her. "I must admit I have been caught off guard by this unexpected Royal command performance request, and had prepared nothing." Guests muttered to each other. "However," she held up her hand, "there is an old air I can present, with a slight modification of the lyrics, in honour of Her Royal Highness, the Queen, who could not be with us this evening." Quiet applause circled the table.

Charlotte sat at the keyboard and played a few notes to get a sense of it. "The tune may be recognizable, but I now call it: 'Portrait of My Grandmother.'" People applauded again.

She began playing a rustic song then sang to it:

> By the canvas may be seen
> How she looked at seventeen,
> As a Bride.
> Beneath a summer tree
> Her fair maiden reverie
> Thrust aside.
>
> Her ringlets are in taste;
> What an arm! and what a waist
> For an arm, it has charm!
> With her bridal-wreath, bouquet,

> White lace farthingale, and gay
> Falbala,—
> If the artist's touch be true,
> What a lucky dog were you,
> Grandpapa!

People snickered at the romantic suggestion.

> Her lips are sweet as love;
> They are parting! Do they move?
> Are they dumb?
> Her eyes are blue, and beam
> So beseechingly, and seem
> To say, "Come!"
>
> What funny fancy slips
> From atween those cherry lips?
> Glory be, whisper me,
> Fairest Sorceress in paint,
> What harsh canon says I mayn't
> Marry thee?
>
> That good-for-nothing Time
> Has a confidence sublime!
> When I first
> Saw this Lady, in my youth,
> All her winters had, forsooth,
> Done their worst.

Guests' jaws dropped as they realised what Charlotte was saying.

> If her voice is rough and gruff,
> 'Tis the snuff, all the snuff,
> Ghastly stuff, quite enough.
> And her locks, now white as snow,
> Once shamed the swarthy crow;
> Me, oh my, by-and-by
> That avenging fowl's black sprite
> Set his cruel foot for spite
> Near her eye.
>
> Ah, what perishable clay!
> As her charms have dropped away

Britain's Glory

> One by one:
> But if she heaves a sigh
> With a burden, it is, "Thy
> Will be done."
>
> Oh, if you could now recur,
> Just as sweet as once you were,
> Grandmama, Grandmama,
> This benighted world agrees
> You would all the better please
> Grandpapa, Grandpapa.

Charlotte stood from the keyboard in silence. After a few seconds, Leopold began clapping and the other guests joined in tepidly. As she sat down next to her husband, he said, "Darling, you sounded great, but I couldn't understand some of the words."

She turned to him and said, "That should teach Prinny not to treat me like a trained monkey on a string."

"Oh, no, my sweet," Leopold sighed. "Were you mocking?"

Instead of answering him, Charlotte turned to the middle-aged man dressed in military formal garb on her other side and inquired, "What did *you* think of 'My Grandmother'?"

He coughed somewhat uncomfortably and replied, "I do believe there was some humour in the piece."

Charlotte retorted, "I do believe there is some very bad humour in *her*!" she giggled. "I don't like that particular piece at all."

5 November 1817, Claremont House, Surrey
Evening

> "At nine o'clock this evening, her Royal Highness the Princess Charlotte was delivered of a still-born male child. Her Royal Highness is doing extremely well." – Progress report from Sir Richard Croft to the Prince Regent

"Charlotte," Leopold whispered, clasping her hand, "we have lost the baby."

"Yes, Leo," she gasped, "I know."

"The physicians tried everything they could think of: mustard, salt rub, immersion in the warm water. Nothing worked."

Croft hovered over Charlotte, eyeing her, palpating her abdomen. He mumbled, "Hourglass," and reached under the blood-filled sheets. Using the tips of his fingers, he pried his way into the constricted uterus and removed the parts of the placenta that would not detach on their own. Instead of pulling the superfluous tissue all the way out, he left it in the birth canal as a plug in order to stop further bleeding. Satisfied with his work, he grabbed a cloth to wipe his hands and began to walk out of the chamber accompanied by the other physicians.

"I am so hungry, so thirsty."

Leopold looked up, "Sir Richard, may she have some nourishment now?"

Husband and wife alone for the first time since this ordeal began, they searched each other's faces for a message. Leopold attempted a smile, Charlotte's eyebrows raised a bit. He squeezed her hand a bit more, realised it was cold and rubbed it with his other hand to bring some warmth.

After a minute the Prince spoke, "I would ask how you feel, but I am fairly certain I already know."

The Princess started to laugh then groaned when her abdomen moved, "It hurts to laugh, Leo. Please be kind. These last few months have been... First my beloved Miss Jane Austen in July, and now this. Too many losses. Too many." She smiled a very pale smile and rubbed her engorged belly. "*Doucement, mon cher, doucement.*"

Leopold smiled at the reprimand. He bent over and kissed her forehead delicately.

Charlotte's nurse, Mrs. Griffiths, entered with a tray of chicken broth and toast with some barley water. She set it on the table near the bed and began to help Charlotte to sit up with Leopold's assistance. Mrs. Griffiths spooned the liquids as the Princess could take them, slowly but gaining strength with each swallow. The Prince stood nearby and watched.

When the Princess had just about finished her meagre meal, Sir Richard returned with a camphor julep for Charlotte. She downed it in one gulp and looked around the room with renewed energy in her eyes.

"How smart you are, Griffiths," Charlotte suddenly spouted, "Why did you not wear my favourite, the silk gown?"

Charlotte: The People's Princess

**Anonymous Poem written for
Princess Charlotte's Twenty-First Birthday**

Whilst with delight I view the blushing morn,
    When Phœbus lights the cheerful lamp of day;
Whose orient beams the eastern world adorn,
    Making all nature blooming, fresh, and gay;

Th' auspicious moment comes into my mind,
    Which, fraught with pleasure, will be treasur'd long
That gave to Charlotte birth, and to mankind
    A theme sublimer than the Muse's song.

Her ripen'd sense with graceful manners join'd,
    In the primeval innocence of youth;
Respects the greatness of a noble mind,
    Replete with knowledge, modesty, and truth.

Her love of liberty, and ardent zeal
    For Britain's Glory and her Sovereign's good,
To all in fairest characters will tell,
    Th' illustrious offspring of great Brunswick's blood.

And while such conduct animates her breast
    In ev'ry gen'rous and each great design,
We see the daughter with those virtues blest
    Which in the Father so transcendent shine.

If genius, wisdom, prudence, can inspire
    Her country with fair virtue's secret charm
Let Charlotte's merits every bosom fire,
    Her worth superior, envy's sting disarm.

May then her Birth-day, source of endless joy
    To noble Coburg and his princely race,
In thoughts propitious ev'ry mind employ,
    And mirth and pleasure smile on ev'ry face.

Prince Leopold

2 May 1817, Claremont House, Surrey
Evening

Most of London society took the trip south to attend the first anniversary party of the Royal Couple. Foreign ambassadors, government functionaries, titled nobles and military heroes. Women wore their high-waisted dresses and Spencer jackets, some lined with lace or fur. Jewelled pins, earrings and necklaces adorned their outfits as well. Feathered headdresses, the current fashion, poked up into the air. The gentlemen wore military garb or tailcoats.

Claremont had modest decorations for the occasion. A few extra crystal candelabras and lamps had been set out. Cloth banners draped the walls and small tables held canapés. The shoulder-height fireplace hearth added a glow and some additional warmth to the drawing room.

Among the guests, one Honourable Margaret Mercer Elphinstone. It was her first visit to Claremont, and despite her custom of being taken directly to see the Princess upon her arrival wherever the Princess might be, this time she was made to wait in line with the other guests to be received by the host and hostess.

"Your Highness," Mercer curtseyed to the Prince and Princess, "Your Highness."

"Countess Flahault," Charlotte responded and bowed ever so slightly.

Mercer raised a silk-gloved hand. "Not quite yet. The nuptials are in a few weeks. You must come."

Remembering how her best friend avoided Charlotte's own wedding, she turned to smile at Leopold as if to get him to understand her reluctance. "Oh, yes, we must!"

"Will we have some time for a private chat later?" Mercer requested.

"Oh, yes, we must!"

Mercer moved along as the queue of people behind her pushed forward.

As soon as Charlotte concluded her duties as hostess welcoming the guests, she sought out Mercer and clasped her hand, leading her into the neighbouensering drawing room.

"M! I have such fantastic news to share!" Charlotte bubbled with enthusiasm.

"Apparently, C, it cannot wait."

"Oh, M, Leopold has given me the most wonderful Birthday gift ever!"

"Are you referring to this anniversary party? Yes, it is most jolly." Mercer glanced about, "Your country home is well-appointed, my dear. Between this and your apartments at Kensington, you appear well-situated."

"Yes, yes, well appointuated," the Princess sputtered. "But, M, that's not the gift I am referring to." She rubbed her abdomen delicately.

"Oh, my, sister C, I do believe you have joined the pudding club." Charlotte smiled a young girl's grin. "My dear, I pray this time you stay in it for the full term. You have been known to drop out at a moment's notice in the past. Perhaps you should sit."

Charlotte flopped into her chair. "Yes, I have had more than my share of miscarriages. In fact–and I have told no one this, you understand–the last was on Christmas Day. I did not want to tell Leopold and disappoint him yet one more time." Mercer nodded somberly. "This is the one, M, this is the one. I just know it!" She struck a valiant pose.

"Of course it is, C, of course it is." Margaret's mind momentarily drifted to her own fear of childbirth and how she will also be expected to produce heirs for her husband-to-be.

"Prinny threw me a Brighton ball for my birthday, but I begged off," Charlotte announced. "I just wasn't ready for public viewing after my Christmas tragedy."

"I have heard it was quite the thing. All of Britain's finest, save you and me, of course." Mercer fanned herself with one hand. "Your private birthday celebration here yielded as much joy with fewer celebrants, I am certain."

"Apparently our private celebration here yielded the necessary magic." She patted her tummy again and they both giggled.

"When is the 'magic' happening?"

"I don't yet know," she stood, threw her hands in the air and then tucked them behind her back in her standard pose. "I meet with the physicians soon, and they shall calculate all of that."

An icy breeze passed through the room, gently plucking the strings of Charlotte's harp, eerily vibrating the strings, tuned to a minor key.

"Have you informed His Regency of the situation?"

Charlotte nodded. "Leopold drove up to Carlton last month to convey the news to Papa. The whole family is excited to have its newest heir."

Mercer glared at the Princess, "You mean its only legitimate heir, don't you?"

Charlotte: The People's Princess

Charlotte gazed upward and dropped her jaw, "With so many aunts and uncles, it is difficult to accept that not a one of them with a sanctioned marriage has children."

"I do believe they expect your Prinny will outlive them all, alleviating them from the pressure to produce royal heirs," Margaret quipped.

Charlotte continued without looking at her friend, "And once I have provided a new generation for them," she stroked her abdomen, "they will have to show me more respect, and I will be able to begin carrying out the people's will in earnest," she mused. "There are so many reforms needed if this monarchy is to survive."

Margaret marveled as the Princess walked around the chamber expounding.

"My own family has used the public's goodwill, building pleasure palaces and lodges, for their own use." Her arms waved about. "I don't want history to judge us for their excesses. I want to make the crown responsible to the masses once more."

"Hold on, Machiavella," Mercer cautioned, "You have two Georges to outlast before anyone is going to offer *you* the Royal Sceptre."

"Grandpapa is old, and Prinny is ill," she turned to face her friend, "It could happen sooner that you might think."

"Or they might live forever. Modern medicine is working against you."

"I suppose I should not wish such bad tidings on my relatives," Charlotte intoned downwardly, "on the anniversary of our marriage," then smiled brightly, "But this is morose chat for such a happy day. Let us rejoin the party, M, before all the food is gone." She began walking back to the hall.

"All hail Queen Charlotte," Mercer said to her friend's back.

Britain's Glory

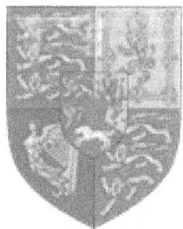

5 November 1817, Claremont House, Surrey
Late evening

The exhausted Princess lay snoring loudly. After an extensive evening of delivering her still-born baby while on starvation, the light meal and camphor julep was welcome refreshment and relaxant. Mrs. Griffith had removed the soiled sheets and replaced them with fresh linens.

"Leo, you should get some rest," Stockmar advised. "I shall stay with Charlotte."

The pacing had started again. "I believe I am too restless for sleep, my friend."

The Baron took a small packet from his coat pocket, emptied the rust-brown powder into a glass of barley water, stirred the mixture with a spoon and handed it to Leopold. "Here, drink this. It will help you sleep."

The Prince stopped briefly to take the draught. When he had finished, he turned to look at his sleeping wife once more. He thought about the ordeal she had endured—they had endured together—over the last three days and realised what a steady soldier she had been. Leopold had been in battle, watched stronger men than him struggle more with fewer hardships. Charlotte had displayed true bottle. Her Brunswick heart had kept her strong. He leaned over the shattered sleeping figure and kissed her forehead one last time before retiring. *Doucement*, he thought, *doucement*. "I suppose I should go to my chambers. Good night, dear Stockmar. Thank you. Thank you for being our friend. Tomorrow shall certainly be a brighter day." He left the chamber.

"Let us all pray that it is, friend."

Just a few moments after Leopold had gone, sounds of wretching came from nearby. A puddle of julep and broth lay on the floor near the Princess.

Charlotte awoke, writhed in the bed, clutching her bloated abdomen, "Oh, what a pain!" she screamed, "It is all here!"

"Mrs. Griffiths! Wake up Sir Richard!" Stockmar ordered.

21 July 1817, Claremont House, Surrey
Afternoon

Charlotte, Leopold and Baron Stockmar sat at the small dining table, awaiting the arrival of Doctor Baillie, the physician appointed by Charlotte's father to oversee the pregnancy.

"After all, you two have been extremely generous with your gifts," Stockmar stated. "It has been noted in London–and the surrounding area. The bibles, the meat, the grain. Very generous, indeed."

The Princess smiled. She wished to be thought of as a benefactor, unlike her elders who were despised because of their self- indulgent grandiose lifestyles.

Leopold looked at his wife and smiled with her, "I do believe it is in everyone's best interest to be..." he looked to Stockmar, "*karitativ?*"

"Charitable, yes. Anything we can do to improve our image works in our favour, Leo."

"I believe you misunderstand me, Stockmar. I want to be generous because it is the right thing to do, not because it will buy friendship and goodwill."

Charlotte stared out the window while the men continued to speak. She was not happy about her father choosing a physician for her, especially because it was Grandpapa's physician. At least she would have her own choice of midwife, as suggested by Lady Ashbrook, the woman who introduced the Princess to the joy of playing harp.

"Leo, you are still naive. These English did not welcome us with joy. Every day we hope to be less an invader and more an ally with these people. I hope you soon realise that."

"I do what I do because the divine master wills it," he squeezed Charlotte's hand gently and she smiled, "And whatever my earthly master says as well," he smiled at Charlotte.

Stockmar turned away, "Oh, you two are too much in love."

"There is no such thing as too much love," Leopold crooned.

Charlotte pointed out the window, "Oh, look! They are arrived," she stated with minimal enthusiasm, as if it were her grandmother come to visit with boiled mutton.

"Doucement, ma chère," Leopold advised, "Doucement."

The three stood and walked to the entry hall. House staff had seen to the entry of the two guests. Charlotte extended her chubby hand slowly, "Doctor Baillie, welcome to Claremont." Her tone suggested a desire to be somewhere else and with someone else.

Doctor Matthew Baillie, Physician Extraordinary to King George III, studied at the University of Glasgow and Oxford then taught anatomy at St. George's Hospital. At this point he was in his late 50s, but still a striking, pale and noble figure. His attitude also suggested a desire to be somewhere else.

The physician took Charlotte's hand and kissed it blandly. "Thank you, Your Highness," he spoke with a slight Scottish brogue, "I wish to present my brother-in-law, Sir Richard Croft."

The Princess then gave her hand to the other guest, who kissed it even more blandly, "Sir Richard."

"Shall we sit?" Stockmar asked and led the group to some chairs in the sitting room nearby. He then signaled to the house staff to bring tea service for the guests.

Dr. Baillie studied Stockmar for a moment, "Baron, are you not a physician as well? I have been informed so. Please tell me if this information is, in fact, speculation."

Stockmar smiled politely, "Yes, it is true that I have received training in the medical arts, but I cater to only one patient, His Most Serene Highness," and he indicated Prince Leopold.

"Then perhaps you would care to join the team attending the Princess during her term."

The Baron held up his hand, "While I appreciate the offer, I must decline. Women's medicine is foreign to me and I would prefer to have more knowledgeable attendants for the Princess." He glanced at Charlotte, who reached over, patted his hand affectionately and then gave it a bit of a hard squeeze.

"As you wish, Baron," the Physician Royal responded.

"Well, Doctor Baillie," Charlotte spurted out, pulling her hand back, "Everyone wants to know the arrival date. Have you the calculations?"

"Yes, Your Highness." He reached inside the woolen overcoat and withdrew a folded piece of paper. "Given the information you have provided, we have calculated that your confinement shall begin 19 October."

"October, Leopold!" She faced her husband, "A jolly month for a child's birthday!"

"I am pleased that Your Highness accepts our calculations," Dr. Baillie continued, "however, that leaves us only a few months to prepare, and we must begin a rigorous programme to ensure the safety of both baby and mother."

"Of course, Doctor," she turned to him, "When do I meet with the accoucheur?"

"You have already met him, Your Highness. Sir Richard is to be your accoucheur."

Charlotte glanced sideways at Croft. "But Lady Ashbrook recommended Sir William Knighton."

"And as your physician, appointed by the Prince Regent, I have decided upon Sir Richard," Dr. Baillie commanded.

"But I know nothing of this man!" She pointed at Croft the way a judge points at the accused. "He is a stranger to me."

"Your Highness, I would not have brought him with me if I did not vouch fully for his capacities. Sir Richard sat at St. Bart's, practiced at Oxford and has attended numerous confinements of noble parents for over 15 years now. A more qualified candidate for this delicate office cannot exist." He patted Croft on the shoulder with confidence.

Charlotte glanced at Leopold and Stockmar. They both nodded their heads in agreement. She grimaced and cast her eyes down. "We shall accept your nominee," and then glared at Dr. Baillie, "but *you* shall have to explain this to Lady Ashbrook upon her return from Rome."

Stockmar turned to Croft, "How do you wish to begin, Sir Richard?"

Charlotte bolted upright and her head snapped to the Baron, eyes afire.

Croft looked at Doctor Baillie for confidence, cleared his throat noisily, and addressed Stockmar, "First off, it is apparent that Her Highness has gained too much weight to be healthy for the sake of herself and the child."

"It's my stout Brunswick constitution," she declared.

Sir Richard regarded Charlotte briefly then looked again at the Baron, "What is Her Highness's usual luncheon?"

"Her Highness usually has..." Stockmar began.

"Her Highness can speak for herself," Charlotte interrupted. "Please address me directly, Sir Richard. There is no need to have an intermediary here. We all speak the same tongue."

"Yes, Your Highness," he squeaked. "I am not in the custom of interacting directly with the mother until the delivery time."

"Well, Sir Richard, we are well into the 19th Century now. Your antiquated manner of treating an expectant mother like a *persona non grata* does not please me at all. I shall speak for myself without the need for a male voice or interpreter."

"Yes, Your Highness." He nodded his head nervously. "Your customary luncheon, Your Highness?"

"A British mutton chop and a glass of port, of course," as if everyone in Great Britain could afford such luxury.

"I see," Croft replied absently, "From here on out it shall be tea with bread and butter. At times, some cold meat and some fruit is acceptable." Charlotte knitted her brow and pursed her lips slightly. "We must bring your weight in line to have a healthy baby."

The Princess bulged her eyes, "You would kill me for the sake of the baby?"

Croft cleared his throat vainly, "Your Highness, it is my professional opinion that an overfed mother is anathema to proper fetal growth."

Charlotte turned to Stockmar, "Stocky, how does Sir Richard's advice sit with you?"

The Baron looked at Baillie, who was staring off into the distance, then at Leopold, who offered no indication. Then he responded, "Princess, male health is my specialty, and women's issues I know very little about. I would suggest following Sir Richard's advice."

She gritted her lips, "If I must."

"And does Her Highness take regular exercise?"

"Oh, yes!" she perked up, "I ride almost every day, hunt a few times a week, and walk to town as often as possible."

"You shall be restricted to a once daily walk about your grounds. Riding can be dangerous, but if you must, it should be no more than once a week and only on days when the ground is suitably hard. No more hunting."

"Leopold... I don't wish to give up my hunting," Charlotte implored.

"We must listen to the doctor, my sweet." She squinted her eyes slightly. "He has the best interests of the baby in mind."

"I do hope I may still take air and make water without restriction." Charlotte affirmed.

"Barley water only henceforth. No more alcohol."

"Following your draconian instructions, I shall pass away from starvation and boredom before the child even arrives." She banged her hand on the chair arm. "This is bloody well ridiculous! You follow your diet and then let us chat."

"Your Highness," Croft's tone bordered on supercilious, "were I a woman with child, I would, but as I am a man, it is not practical."

Charlotte glared at him with one eye.

"I have hired a practical nurse for you, a Mrs. Griffiths. She is well-acquainted with my methods and shall arrive in a month's time. Until then, I shall count on the house staff to carry out my orders. Where is the scullery? I wish to address your cooking staff."

Leopold pointed toward the door leading to the kitchen. Croft and Baillie stood and walked into the next room.

For half a minute the three sat in silence.

Leopold spoke at last, "Stocky, why on earth did you decline to serve with the physicians? It is my wish that you did. I do not trust them."

"My dear Leopold, if I became part of their team, any merit of mine would be quickly forgotten. Any detriment, even if it were not my fault, would be hung about my neck for all eternity."

Charlotte: The People's Princess

The two doctors returned. Croft stopped in front of a half-finished portrait of Charlotte. "I have given instruction to your staff. Who is the painter?" He pointed at the portrait.

"Sir Thomas Lawrence. Why?"

"Are you wearing stays while posing, Your Highness?"

"Of course," Charlotte responded, "it is the standard. Sir Thomas has allowed for it."

"I forbid it," Croft ordered, and the Princess glanced askew at him, "Being forced to hold your pose and remain in one position for a prolonged period will do harm to the baby. A cow does not wear stays. Why should the Princess Charlotte?"

5 November 1817, Claremont House, Surrey
Night

Charlotte convulsed, slowly at first. Her chest spasmed and her breathing became rapid and shallow.

The Baron looked at Sir Richard, who merely stood observing his patient as if he were waiting for her to tell him what was wrong. Unable to abide this apparent lack of interest, Stockmar grabbed Charlotte's hand professionally, "Charlotte, stay with us." He turned to Croft, "Give her something to stop this!"

The Princess started rolling from side to side. Stockmar released his grip but remained beside her and attempted to provide comfort as best he could.

Sir Richard prepared a drink and stepped to the bed with a cup. The two physicians watched the Princess writhe and contort, knowing there was nothing they could do to improve the situation.

A few minutes passed and Charlotte began to calm. When it became apparent that the convulsions had subsided, Sir Richard handed her the cup.

"Is there any danger?" Charlotte rasped.

Croft responded, "Not if Your Highness composes herself and lies still."

She glanced at Stockmar, who was glaring at Sir Richard, then sipped at the warm, dark liquid. When she finished, she dropped the cup and fell back to the bed.

Stockmar monitored Charlotte for a few moments to assure himself that she was still breathing then asked "Croft, what was that?"

"A bit of laudanum, brandy and hot wine. She should rest easily now."

29 October 1817, Claremont House, Surrey
Afternoon

Dusty rays of sun shone through the windows, coating Charlotte, Leopold and Stockmar in dappled light. The three sat at the dining table finishing their luncheon. The men had sliced pheasant in gravy, potatoes and country bread. The Princess had a cold, thin slice of mutton, dry toast and barley water. Leopold sipped at his sherry.

Charlotte groaned and looked around the drawing room, "19 October has bloody well come and gone!" She pushed the dry piece of meat around her plate with a slice of toast. "I can no longer tolerate such an impossible gravid condition! Will this baby ever arrive?" She dropped the bread and studied the scarred backs of her hands.

Despite the "lowering" regimen imposed by Sir Richard Croft, the Princess continued to gain weight, much to the dismay of her grandmother the Queen, who had delivered 15 babies without adding unnecessary pounds. Some people had expressed the feeling Charlotte might be carrying twins, due to her size. Physicians had difficulty locating veins for bleeding; the back of her hand had to be used.

"My dearest," cooed Leopold, "You won't have to wait much longer," he glanced over at Stockmar, "Isn't that right, Baron?"

Stockmar nodded obligingly.

"The family is now planning a holiday in Bath," she held up a letter, "I wish I could be joining them instead of being forsaken here like some brooding farm animal." The term 'brooding' also seemed to match her mood.

"Stockmar and I shall never leave your side, my dearest."

"Even my own mother cannot pause her cavorting about the Continent long enough to see me through."

Stockmar understood that in the late stages of pregnancy, especially after the estimated confinement date had passed, a mother-to-be could be somewhat irritable. "The finished portrait is beautiful, Charlotte," he attempted.

"I look fat! The only thing that portrait was good for was building up my muscles!"

"Patience, my dear." Leopold attempted to comfort her. "Perhaps a stroll or ride would help. I would be happy to go with you."

"I went yesterday. Sir Richard forbids me to go two days in a row."

Stockmar suggested, "I'll go get the playing cards and we can give Karnöffel a go."

Charlotte looked at him with just a hint of malice.

"Baron," Leopold spoke up, hoping to hit upon an acceptable subject, "have you heard what happened at Wartburg last week?" The Princess perked up at the potential for political discussions.

"No, Leo," Stockmar replied, "what happened at Wartburg?"

"Students marched to the castle to support unification of the German Confederation. They burned some books and other symbolic objects." Charlotte smiled at her husband, hoping for some distraction to take her mind off the current situation. "They want to destroy things they do not like."

"Such as?" the Baron inquired.

"Oh, I hear it was anything to do with Napoleon or the Napoleonic Code."

"That makes sense," Stockmar nodded and Charlotte agreed, "This is about the time of year they defeated Napoleon."

"But the books were political tracts and religious treaties they did not agree with," Leopold continued. "One cannot destroy ideas by merely destroying paper."

"That is very true, my love," the Princess stated. "But as we have seen over the last few decades, the world is beginning to move away from a monarchy-based government system."

Both men looked at Charlotte simultaneously.

"This is a new Century and a new World. Starting with the breakaway of the Colonies in America—which my grandfather has never recovered from—and the French uprising following that." She was now energised, having a topic to discuss with her two men. "The German Confederation may want to unify, but it may not be a *König* or *Kaiser* they are after."

Leopold and Stockmar looked at each other.

"What is it with the two of you?" Charlotte posed. "Your thinking is from the *last* Century. The world, and the England over which I will preside, in all probability will not be administered by kings or dictators, but by representative governance."

The Prince and the Baron re-examined the Princess with discerning glances.

"And women are increasingly more equal, more powerful, no longer condemned to the gloomy shadows of politics. I want this baby," she continued while gently caressing her

Charlotte: The People's Princess

huge tummy, "to have every available opportunity, many of which I have been denied."

Charlotte turned to Leopold, "People already consider me the hope of this nation, and that added burden of expectation will most assuredly be passed along." She paused to breathe audibly. "Besides, by the time our child ascends the throne, there may not even be a throne to sit upon."

The men once again turned their heads to face each other.

"After all, during the Commonwealth period the populace took governing into its own hands for a time." She fiddled with her beheaded ancestor's sapphire. "I fear that if my family does not rein in its appetite for grandeur, well... who knows..." She rubbed her neck with one hand and placed the other on the table next to her.

The men looked at Charlotte again.

"I do hope no such incident like that ever happens here," and she laid one hand on top of the other, "again."

A minute passed without conversation.

"I am still pregnant. Nothing seems to have changed." She patted her enlarged abdomen.

"The time will come, Charlotte," Stockmar advised, "the time is near. I am sure of it."

Charlotte nodded and muttered, "*Espérance et constance. Espérance et constance.*"

Leopold inquired, "What, my dear?"

"Nothing, Leopold, nothing."

Britain's Glory

Drawing based on the 1817 Portrait
by Sir Thomas Lawrence

5 November 1817, Claremont House, Surrey
Late night

Baron Stockmar woke to Sir Richard Croft patting his hand and shaking it gently. "Baron, the bleeding has started again. I feel it is best if we wake His Highness. Please retrieve him."

A groggy Stockmar made his way to the Prince's chamber only to find him fast asleep and unrousable. Leopold continued to snore despite all attempts made by the Baron. The draught he provided earlier had proven all too effective.

In the birthing room, Croft touched the Princess and found her cold. Her chest rose and fell with unusual noises, more rapid than normal. Not wanting to lose the mother after losing the child, he applied warm compresses to her abdomen in hopes of restoring her body heat. The remains of placenta had fallen completely out as the bleeding continued and increased.

Standard medical procedure in such a situation was to apply cold in order to staunch the bleeding. Warmth only encourages blood flow.

Charlotte: The People's Princess

When Baron Stockmar returned, Charlotte looked up at him with bleary eyes. "They have made me tipsy!" she whispered raspily.

He grasped her delicate wrist and tested her pulse. It was weak and rapid. Her breathing became noisier and rattly.

Sensing that the Princess did not have much time left, Stockmar turned to take leave and make another attempt at rousing the Prince.

Charlotte grabbed his arm with her last energy and croaked, "Stocky! Stocky!" Her body violently contracted into a fetal position and her breathing ceased.

The Baron stood holding the clammy hand of the dead princess while a line of tears trickled down his cheek.

Britain's Glory

THE FUNERAL PROCESSION OF THE PRINCESS CHARLOTTE AT WINDSOR

Daughter of England! for a nation's sighs,
A nation's heart went with thine obsequies!—
And oft shall Time revert a look of grief
On thine existence, beautiful and brief.

They shall describe thy life, thy form pourtray;
But all the love that mourns thee swept away.
'Tis not in language or expressive arts
To paint—ye feel it, Britons, in your hearts.

**From "Monody of the Princess Charlotte"
By Thomas Campbell**

Epilogue

The London Gazette
EXTRAORDINARY

From Whitehall, Thursday November 6, 1817

HER ROYAL HIGHNESS the Princess Charlotte Augusta, daughter of his Royal Highness, the Prince Regent, and consort of his Serene Highness the Prince Leopold of Saxe-Coburg, was delivered of a still-born male child at nine o'clock last night; and, about half-past twelve her Royal Highness was seized with great difficulty of breathing, restlessness, and exhaustion, which alarming symptoms increased till half-past two this morning, when her Royal Highness expired, to the inexpressible grief of his Royal Highness the Prince Regent, of her illustrious Consort the Prince Leopold, and of all the Royal Family.

Mourning began as soon as news reached the people. Two generations of royal succession gone in a night. Prince Leopold sat with the body of his wife for days. The entire British nation lingered under a fog of grief that lasted months. Buildings draped in black displayed the likenesses of Charlotte and Leopold. A charity fund for a marble tribute catalogued one young child giving sixpence. Mother and child lay at Windsor.

Sir Richard Croft, racked with guilt over the deaths, shot himself at the home of a patient the following February.

The race for a royal heir initiated a spate of Regent-approved marriages. The first Royal to produce a child was Prince Edward, the Duke of Kent, who married Leopold's widowed sister Victoria in May 1818. Princess Alexandrina Victoria arrived a year later. Although fifth in line for the crown at birth, she outlived her grandfather George III, her uncle George IV, her uncle William IV, and her father, who died before William. Princess Victoria, crowned Queen in 1837, served the nation until her death in 1901.

When territories of French Walloon and Dutch Flanders united to form the new country of Belgium in 1831, Leopold became its first king. Until his death in 1865, he served as international diplomat and personal advisor to his niece, Queen Victoria, including arranging a marriage for her with his nephew Albert.

Had Charlotte survived and all other circumstances remained the same, she would have become Queen upon the death of her father in 1830.

In May 2015, the current monarch's grandson, Prince William, and his wife, Catherine, Duchess of Cambridge, named their second child Princess Charlotte Elizabeth Diana. This was said to honor both the Prince Charles of Wales, the baby's grandfather, and the subject of this book. May the new Princess Charlotte have a long and healthy life.

Glossary

Accession – The installation of Prince George as Regent without restrictions.
Accoucheur – Male midwife.
Bartholemew Fair – A multi-day event usually held in August for merchants. All classes attended.
Beau Brummel – Gentleman who introduced dark tailored coats and pants in society fashion, initiating what became the modern men's suit.
Boodle's / White's – Gentlemen's clubs in London where upper class men dined.
Bottle – Slang for bravery.
Brighton – A beachside resort town approximately 50 miles south of London.
Buckingham (the Queen's House) – Originally built by the Duke of Buckingham in 1705, King George III purchased it in 1761 for his Queen, Charlotte. It has been greatly improved upon and expanded, and it has served as the Monarch's London residence since 1837.
Chamberlen device – Obstetrical forceps designed by Peter Chamberlen in the early 17th Century.
Charing Cross – The junction of Strand, Whitehall and Cockspur Streets, it is essentially the centre of London. "Cross" refers to the memorial wooden cross placed by Edward I in honour of his dead queen, Eleanor of Castile. Since 1765, a statue of Charles I on horseback occupies the spot.
Charles I – Beheaded in 1649 following Civil War and a trial, he had been accused of using the resources of the kingdom for his own personal desires.

Christopher Wren – British architect noted for helping to rebuild London after the Great Fire of 1666. His most famous work is St. Paul's Cathedral.

Confinement – the period, usually starting with the onset of labour contractions, when a pregnant woman was confined to her bed to prevent premature delivery.

Cranbourne Lodge – Originally the gamekeeper's lodge at Windsor Castle, the house sits at the edge of Great Windsor Park.

Dido – Queen of Carthage. She committed suicide by falling onto the sword of her beloved Æneas, who left her and sailed for Rome as instructed by the gods.

Dragoon – a cavalryman, usually armed with a rifle.

Earl Grey – Charles Grey II, leader of the Whigs and later Prime Minister.

Elphinstone – Admiral George Keith Elphinstone commanded ships of war for Britain, helping to defeat Napoleon's navy. The father of Margaret Mercer Elphinstone.

Esher – The Surrey town approximately 14 miles southwest of London where Charlotte lived with Leopold.

Falbala – Decorative trim, gathered into a ruffle.

Farthingale – Framework used under skirts to create volume and shape. Later replaced by crinoline.

Father Christmas – The British equivalent of Santa Claus.

Guelph – Family name of the Hanovers.

Hanover – Line of British Monarchs starting with George I in 1714. The House of Hanover began in Germany in 1636. When Queen Anne (House of

Stuart) died, she had no heirs and George I (her second cousin) was the closest relative. He spoke no English.

Hussar – Light cavalryman used for scouting and minor skirmishes.

Hyde Park – A large urban park within London. Its main thoroughfare, The King's Private Road, is known as Rotton Road (perhaps from *Route du Roi*, the king's road).

Jack Sheppard – A notorious thief famed for escaping prison many times.

Karnöffel – Card game. A predecessor of modern Cribbage.

Laudanum – Preparation of opium used as a strong analgesic.

Mama – Pronounced muh-MAH, as opposed to MAH-muh.

Mayfair – A district in central London with exclusive shops and luxury hotels.

Merlin chair – Hand-operated wheelchair with two larger wheels behind and one small wheel in front below the footboard. The design was based on the popular Bath Chair used at the resort as a replacement for walking.

Newgate – A prison in the heart of London that held the likes of authors Daniel Defoe and Ben Johnson, statesman William Penn and notorious thief and escape artist Jack Sheppard.

Nibs – British slang for a self-important person.

Nosegay – A small bouquet of flowers, usually placed on the wrist, used to overcome unwanted odors.

Old Bailey – The Central Criminal Court in London.

Pall Mall – A major thoroughfare near St. James Palace, named for a stick-and-ball game once played there.

Papa – Pronounced puh-PAH, as opposed to PAH-puh.

Pelisse – High-waisted, floor-length women's garment, usually made of silk, with military styling, frequently employing frog closures.

Prinny – Nickname for Charlotte's father, Prince George.

Privy Council – A group of advisors to the Monarch. One function the Council performed was witnessing Royal births to attest the authenticity of the children.

Procession of Mail Coaches – Traditional parade in honour of the Monarch's birthday.

Pudding Club – British idiom for pregnancy.

Pulteney Hotel – On the corner of Bolton and Piccadilly, north of Green Park in London, it was the first hotel to have flush toilets.

Quoz – A Cockney sentiment of exasperation popular around 1800.

St. James Palace – Built by Henry VIII on the site of a former leper hospital dedicated to St. James the Less, it was used as the London residence of George III. Whitehall Palace was the previous Royal residence until it burned in 1691.

Sandhurst Military Academy – The British Royal Military Academy, approximately 34 miles southwest of London.

Spencer jacket – A rib-length woolen coat named for the Second Earl Spencer.

Stage Box – A phrase uttered by an audience when desiring to see the royals in attendance.

The Peace – End of military engagement between Great Britain and Napoleonic France at the beginning of the 19th Century.

Thomas Bruce – The Seventh Earl of Elgin. While serving as the British Ambassador to the Ottoman Empire, he negotiated a contract with Sultan Selim III to purchase several of the marble pieces from the Parthenon on the Acropolis of Athens.

Tory – British political party that favoured the Monarchy and noble classes. Conservative in nature, they worked to maintain the rule of the landed gentry.

Vienna Congress – Political committee drawn up to settle national borders following the defeat of Napoleon.

Wartburg Castle – Near Eisinach, Germany. Martin Luther hid at the castle during the time he translated the New Testament into German.

Whig – British political party that favoured the rule of Parliament over the Monarch. Their focus was on the betterment of the working class and are deemed Liberal.

William Pitt (the Younger) – Prime Minister of Britain 1783-1801 and 1804-06. His father, William Pitt (the Elder) had previously served as Prime Minister.

Windsor – The castle originally built by William the Conqueror, approximately 25 miles west of London. Expanded and improved over the years, it has served as the Royal residence and retreat.

BIBLIOGRAPHY

Ackroyd, Peter, *London: the Biography* (Anchor Books, New York, 2001)

Chambers, James, *Charlotte & Leopold* (Old St. Publishing, London, 2007)

Gill, Gillian, *We Two, Victoria and Albert: Rulers, Partners, Rivals* (Ballantine Books, New York, 2009)

Hamilton, Edwin B. *A Record of the Life and Death of Her Royal Highness, the Princess Charlotte* (Unknown, 1817)

Huish, Robert, *Memoirs of Her Late Royal Highness Charlotte Augusta, Princess of Wales and Saxe-Coburg* (Thomas Kelly, London, 1818)

Jones, C. Rachel and Herbert, *The Princess Charlotte of Wales* (Wyman & Sons, London, 1885)

Knight, Cornelia, *Autobiography of Miss Cornelia Knight, Lady Companion to the Princess Charlotte of Wales* (W.H. Allen & Co., London, 1861)

Lethbridge, Ann, *Princess Charlotte's Choice* (Harlequin, Don Mills, Ontario, Canada, 2011)

Pearce, Charles C., *The Beloved Princess* (Stanley Paul & Co., London, 1911)

Perceval, Spencer, *An Inquiry or Delicate Investigation into the Conduct of Her Royal Highness the Princess of Wales* (W. Lindsell, London, 1813)

Weigall, Rose, *A Brief Memoir of the Princess Charlotte of Wales* (John Murray, London, 1874)

Williams, Kate, *Becoming Queen Victoria* (Ballantine Books, New York, 2008)

--*A Biographical Memoir of the Much Lamented Princess Charlotte Augusta of Wales and Saxe-Coburg, Fourth Edition* (J. Barfield, London, 1818)

—*The Life and Memoirs of Her Royal Highness, Princess Charlotte of Saxe, Coburg, Saalfeld, &c.* (J. McGowan, London, 1821)

—*Memoirs of the Late Princess Charlotte Augusta of Wales and Saxe-Coburg* (Robert Desilv, Philadelphia, 1818)

ISBN: 978-0-9888143-1-8

Library of Congress Control Number: 2013905078
© 2012, W. Goodman

WAYNE GOODMAN has lived in the San Francisco Bay Area most of his life (with too many cats). When not writing, he enjoys playing Gilded Age parlor music on the piano, with an emphasis on women, gay, and Black composers.

Other Books by
Wayne Goodman

THE LAST GREAT HOPE

A retired Secret Service agent, with a secret of his own, is called up for one last mission: Find the long-lost child of John and Jacqueline Kennedy, whom he adopted out unknowingly under orders of his power-hungry boss.

THE SEED OF IMMORTALITY

Three great philosophies and a mythological blue dragon lead a peasant and his conniving friend on a series of adventures throughout Ancient China. Along the way they visit the Great Wall, sail down the Yangtze, and have an audience with the first Emperor in his mysterious subterranean palace.

www.ingramcontent.com/pod-product-compliance
Lightning Source LLC
Chambersburg PA
CBHW052023290426
44112CB00014B/2349